Com... My Soul

*Essays from a Fishing Nut
Navigating Family Life*

Matt Reinemo

Acknowledgements

I would like to thank Anne Phanuef, perhaps the only copy editor willing to be paid with a fishing trip.

I would like to thank Spider Andresen and Flip Pallot, men at the pinnacle of the angling world, who are kind and generous with their time.

I would like to thank my aunt Meg Ruley for her continued support and guidance in the world of publishing.

I would like to thank my aunts, Joanne Skokan and Rosie Atkins, my uncle, Bob Ruley, and my friend, Jake Forgit, for their editing and suggestions.

I would like to once again thank my best friends and in-laws, Charlie and Ruthie Walsh, for their generosity with time and babysitting.

I would like to thank my friend Toph Gorab for editing and suggestions, access to his impressive photo library, including the jumping sailfish on the cover, and timely help with many little tasks along the way.

Thanks to all my clients, especially Erik Passanante and Bill Palmer, and my friend Mike Schuster, who make going to work a pleasure and a treat.

And a very special thanks to my wife, Liz, my son, Chick, and my daughter, Vivi, for everything.

This book is dedicated to my mother and father,
Julie and Karsten Reinemo.

*Thank you for the exceptional parenting, in fishing and
otherwise. I failed to realize how difficult your job is, or how
wonderful you are at it, until I had to do it myself.*

Contents

1

Enchanted Sandbar

A Fishing Nut Wins The Geographic Lottery

Nantucket was recently named National Geographic's best island in the world. Upon hearing the news, most Nantucketers felt like we had won something. Those of us inclined to trash-talking felt like yelling at Fiji, Tahiti, St. Barth's, and especially Martha's Vineyard, "Who is the best island now, bitches!" or something along those lines. When I stopped to think about it though, what was won? There was surely no prize money or trips to one of the runners-up for Nantucket residents. The ranking was completely arbitrary and totally meaningless, and upon further thought it registered as vaguely disappointing because it may attract more people. Despite my charms and the charms of my neighbors, the people did not make it the best island in the world and more of them will inevitably screw it up.

Though we didn't win anything, maybe Nantucketers enjoyed the announcement because it reminded us that we had already won. We didn't win when the article came out in National Geographic, we won when we chose to live here, or in my case, I won by being born here. People's passion for the island felt validated, whatever they see was being seen, being recognized, by the public at large, or if not the public at large, by at least one magazine writer possessing a familiarity with islands.

In that respect it was not all bad. Despite fueling my fear about more people coming here, it served as a nice reminder that I am a very lucky and very happy guy, living in what could be considered paradise. I like to think that is not something I take for granted, but a reminder now and then cannot hurt. That is not to say my life is and has been free of struggles or tragedy. There are and have been both, and while I decline to pass judgment on whether or not I have endured my share, or more than my share, I assure you I am not skirting them altogether. Nevertheless, sometimes I feel like a number of longshots came through for me. On top of Liz and Chick, who are tops, I have a caring family and cherished friends. Just that short and important list should be enough to make any man happy, but my icing on the cake is that I am nuts about fishing and I live on Nantucket.

Sometimes, I think about the math involved in putting me where I am. According to some extremely shoddy internet research and a little math, it seems that a little more than 124 million people shared my birth year. On average more than 340,000 people were born per day. Of those 340,000 and change, only one was born on Nantucket, and it was me. The odds swell drastically when you figure that even today a baby is not born every day on Nantucket, and there was certainly not a baby-per-day in 1980. Perhaps another, even simpler way to look at it would be that ballpark, there are seven billion people in the world and ten thousand on Nantucket, making me one in seven hundred thousand. The numbers can be fiddled with any which way, and perhaps statisticians will find flaws, but the actual numbers are beside the point. The point is, that the moment I was born, I won the geographic lottery.

I am not saying Nantucket is the best place in the world, regardless of National Geographic rankings, and every other place is inferior. In fact, if my passion were any number of other things, skiing for example, Nantucket would be a shitty place to live. The nearest mountain is, at the very least, a boat or plane ride and a significant drive away. Every time you want to hit the slopes, you need to take a vacation. The point is that I am a fishing nut, and I was born on this enchanted sandbar surrounded by the Atlantic, smack dab in the middle of some world-class fishing. It is like being a skiing nut born in Lake Tahoe, a fashion nut being born in New York (or wherever else fashion comes from), a trout nut born in Montana or a lover of peaches and peanuts born in Georgia.

In response to this observation, one could argue it was not a stroke of luck at all: I am not a fishing nut who *happened* to born on Nantucket, I am a fishing nut *because* I was born on Nantucket. That may be right, perhaps I am a product of my environment, nurture over nature. Perhaps if I were born at the foot of the Rockies, I would be a skier; at Pebble Beach, I would be an enthusiastic golfer; in Western Pennsylvania I would be a great quarterback; in Kentucky I would be enthralled with horses. But even a quick look at my friends and acquaintances from high school proves that by no means does growing up here make you an angler. Over the past several years, my classmate and friend Kevin Conrad has become a dedicated and passionate angler, a dogged pursuer of big game, and our classmates Brian Hudzik and Keith Day get out as much a they can, but I think that is about it. My buddies Travis and John are natural athletes and have accompanied me on enough trips that now a rod is comfortable in their hands, but by their own admission they are surely not dedicated anglers. Many islanders do not even own a rod, and many who do don't know how to use it. And these non-anglers are not unique to Nantucket. I have met scores of people from Miami and even the Keys with no interest in fishing, despite the dozens of highly sought after species and year-round availability fish right in their backyards. The Outer Banks, Montana, the Bahamas, Costa Rica, and all the world-class fishing destinations around the globe are populated to some degree by non-anglers.

The opposite it true as well. It doesn't take a home amongst great fishing to make a passionate angler. My buddy Murph became a fly fisherman on the streams of Maryland and Virginia while living in Washington, DC, after leaving Nantucket. My excellent friend and client Erik Passanante has become a total fishing nut, his passion growing exponentially from his home in Darien, Connecticut. Many of my clients are passionate anglers, waiting and planning and looking forward to their time on the water, while spending the great majority of their time in cities miles and miles away from any fishable water. There are plenty of anglers out there whose passion sprouted from lots of time on mediocre water close to home, or perhaps on a brief trip to good water, or some combination of the two, but certainly, one does not need to be from a world-class fishing spot to become a fishing nut.

You do need some time on the water, and certainly that time is a little easier to come by if you are from a fishing town, or at least a town where fishing takes place. If and when that time on the water comes, some will be bored, or fail to see the point, and they will not fish again. To be honest, I suspect people in this group have some kind of mental defect, but it is a distinct possibility that my constant preoccupation with fishing is not the pinnacle of sanity, and I try not to judge.

Some people, in fact probably most, will find fishing anywhere from satisfactory to a hell of a lot of fun, and will fish again if and when they get the opportunity, becoming anything from a tourist who wets a line a few times a decade when on vacation to a bona fide angler who fishes weekends when time allows, owns some tackle and perhaps even a boat, and perhaps even travels occasionally with the goal to catch fish.

Then there is the person who gets from fishing an untouchable something, wonderful, exhilarating, difficult and downright magical. They not only fish at every reasonable opportunity and many unreasonable ones, but they become immersed in the culture. They become fishing nuts. Fishing magazines and catalogs arrive in the mailbox, and gear starts to accumulate. My longtime client and close friend Bill Palmer has a brother who is devout bluewater guy. Bill told me the last time he was at his brother's house, he inquired of his brother whether Shimano was using his basement as a warehouse. I found this funny, not only because it is absurd, but particularly because this specific brand of absurdity is common in my circles. My basement is packed with all manner of tackle and I have recently expanded to a shed. My wife would go bananas, but she is an incurable collector of useless decorative knick-knacks, trinkets, and do-dads, and therefore lacks standing to complain about basement storage. My friend and fellow charter captain Josh Eldridge recently offered to sell me a couple nice rods at an excellent price. I assumed he was not planning to give up angling and I was surprised. I asked him why he wanted to part with them. I learned he had recently cleaned his shop (his tackle having swelled out of his basement long ago) and had counted 127 rods. After considering all the fishing possibilities and contingencies in the near future, he felt comfortably equipped with only 125, and was willing to part with two.

In addition to the accumulation of gear, non-fishing obligations are strenuously limited and those that cannot be avoided are planned so as to not conflict with the best times and tides. Vacations become fishing trips to places with more plentiful fish, bigger fish, or different fish than what you find at home. Day dreaming becomes a persistent problem; even when you are at home or work your mind is watching a big teaser bubble just outside the prop wash, the mountains of Costa Rica's Osa Peninsula off to your left and nothing but the blue Pacific on your right, or perhaps you find yourself on a white sand flat in the Bahamas looking at a quivering tail, half out of the water, just before you make a cast. Then your wife yells at you to pay attention, but even once you are violently jolted back to your living room, you spend your lucid moments trying to decide whether your next vacation should be spent in that Costa Rica bluewater or on the Bahamian flats, and how you are going to go about finding the time and money to do either.

As a member of the last group, a total fishing nut, I am happy and thankful to also be a Nantucketer. Perhaps I am a product of my environment, and perhaps of chemical make-up, and most likely some mixture of the two, but in the end it really does not matter too much. I am a fishing nut and I live surrounded by the Atlantic Ocean.

My proximity to fishing is excellent. If I find myself with a few spare hours, even at the last minute, I can be fishing within minutes with almost no prior planning. A fishing trip for me does not have to be an all-day affair; it can be an any-day affair. While that is wonderful, and should not be taken for granted, by no means is my situation unique. Some fortunate folks have their own dock right outside their door, or a stream running through their land, or a pond in their backyard. My father owns a small home with a dock on a canal in Pine Island, Florida. After fishing there, coming home and having to first get in the car and drive to the boat seems a nearly insurmountable inconvenience. For those without direct access, I am hardly alone in being able to be fishing quickly. Plenty of people live within a walk or drive of some fishing. Even urbanites can often find some angling close to home. I just read Ian Frazier's *The Fish's Eye*, in which he rides the New York City subway to some stripers. But out my door, the fishing is great. I am not saying that Nantucket is hands down the greatest fishing spot in the world anymore than I am saying it is the greatest spot in the world, but I have fished in a lot of spots all over the world, and without a doubt much of what Nantucket has to offer is world-class.

Our striper fishing is consistent and superb. We lie right in the path of their migration, and we are far enough North that they stick around all summer. Cool currents influence the waters east of the island and good striper fishing can be had there even in the midst of summer. I have never tried to find bluefish anywhere other than Nantucket, but I would have a hard time believing there is a better place to find them on earth. The aggressive, acrobatic, hard pulling blues are usually happy to oblige the angler even when the stripers are reticent. Bonito become available consistently in the late summer, and false albacore visit in the fall. Excellent bottom fishing for fluke, black sea bass and scup is also available inshore. Offshore to the east lie some of the best of bluefin tuna grounds in the world. Offshore to the south can offer a smorgasbord of warm-water species, and it was once very good swordfish and white marlin territory, with the marlin making a promising comeback over the last couple years. Nantucket is a dream destination for many anglers, and certainly a worthy one, and I get to reap the benefits without any travel.

Often the realization of how good I have it comes not while enjoying great fishing around Nantucket, but tough fishing somewhere else. Off the cuff, I would guess that I have been skunked as many times fishing elsewhere as I have on Nantucket, and given that upwards of ninety percent of my fishing is out of Nantucket, those are good odds. Much of that is due to the fact that I am experienced and full of local knowledge in Nantucket, whereas anywhere else I am, at best somewhat familiar, and often a fumbling newbie. It is also in part due to the voracious appetite of the bluefish and their predilection for Nantucket's waters. Regardless, Nantucket is not just an excellent place to cast a rod, it is an excellent place to *bend* a rod. Living on Nantucket, I am not a fisherman who always wants to be somewhere else, where the fishing is better. I only want to be somewhere else part of the time, which as a fisherman, and perhaps as a human, is about the best you can hope for.

Obviously my chief complaint about Nantucket is the existence of winter, which I dislike to some degree due to the cold and much more so due to the unavailability of gamefish. I spend large chunks of time in the winter wishing I was somewhere else, but from roughly May through October there is no place I would rather be, and in fact, one of my standing goals is to avoid any travel (especially non-fishing travel) during those months. If I lived, just for instance, next door to my buddy Toph in Sparta, New Jersey, I would spend the winter wishing I lived in southern latitudes among billfish or bonefish and I would spend the summer wishing I lived on Nantucket. I love New Jersey and I hate to pick on the much-maligned state. I attended college there and feel it is one of the most underrated states in the union, complete with some world-class fishing of its own, but nevertheless, I would spend most of my time there wishing I were elsewhere.

Despite Nantucket's charms I have often considered relocation, or at least a seasonal migration. The charms of a tropical locale are never far from my mind (for at least five months a year). In my twenties I suppose it was a search for a job as much as anything else, even the best fishing guides in the Northeast find themselves unemployed for about six months a year, and substantially under-employed for another two or three. If I were to scrape a living together sportfishing, heading south for at least a portion of my year was a necessity. Aside from a few months in Costa Rica, decent winter sportfishing employment never materialized.

Even without employment, a Norman Paperman-type escape beckoned. I looked at ads for charter boats or operations for sale in the tropics. I thought about running the *Topspin* south. I had all kinds of daydreams and schemes, almost all of which my father had the good sense to shoot down. Whatever financial security I have today is largely in part due to his advice against sportfishing investments in developing countries. I had the freedom, but I didn't have any money. When I had a little money, it did not seem like enough. Just when it looked like I may be able to pull of some kind of seasonal migration, I met Liz. Now, with a wife and son, relocation or migration is highly unlikely.

I wonder if things would have been different if I was not born on Nantucket. If I had been born in Springfield, Massachusetts, or Easton, Pennsylvania, would I have picked up stakes and made my way to Costa Rica or Belize or the Florida Keys? Would good year-round fishing have been enough to motivate a pilgrimage then, having limited fishing in my backyard? I think it probably would have been, and looking back, I suppose I certainly have not been a homebody. There were plenty of missed opportunities in my twenties, to be sure, but my twenties are much more a story of fun, experience and substantial folly rather than missed opportunities and a life unlived. Now that the time has come to set down roots, I have chosen to set those roots in my hometown. I do not have to, and never had to, make the difficult decision to uproot my life. The fact that my hometown does not offer year-round saltwater fishing is perhaps not ideal, but six months of paradise is not tough to take. I do not have to decide whether to live in my hometown, or live close to my passion. I have already made decisions regarding my career, that being to totally forsake any real one for the time being, and to cobble together a living from guiding, scalloping, and perhaps writing.

But, for instance, if fisheries managers do not take their heads out of their asses, and striped bass populations continue to plummet, leaving the entire Northeast without their premier gamefish, will I pack things up and head south? Who knows, it is easier said than done. Chick is the thirteenth generation of my family to be born on Nantucket. Our family tree goes back all

15

the way to Tristram Coffin and the first boat of white settlers that came over. We have a pretty good thing going. Packing it up and leaving would not be easy, and as long as fishing stays good, I don't suppose it will be necessary. Maybe even that would not be enough, my ancestors stuck around even after whaling went in the toilet, and perhaps I would stick too.

Perhaps whatever makes me a Nantucketer, and keeps me here, runs deeper than I think. On the other hand, maybe there is something in me or in Chick from our great-many-times-over grandfather Tristram. It is buried under many generations, but it is there. It brought him to Nantucket in the first place. The intrepid courage to sail over the horizon, have an adventure, to search for a better life. I don't need it or want it right now, but you never know when it may come in handy. Maybe the billionaires, wanna-be billionaires, fisheries managers, spineless politicians, readers of National Geographic, and a whole host of incompetent nincompoops will conspire to ruin this grand place and I will need that intrepid courage to move on, preferably to someplace that not enough people know about for it to rate a mention in National Geographic's next rankings. Or perhaps Chick's passions will simply lie elsewhere and he will need it.

But I hope not. I hope that long after everyone forgets about the silly article, all I will need, and maybe even all Chick will need, is a calm morning in June floating somewhere between Madaket and Tuckernuck, in the company of striped bass, to be reminded that life, as a fishing nut on this enchanted sandbar, is pretty sweet.

2

Chick's Arrival & the Consequential Variation on the Compass of My Soul

I got out of school yesterday, hopped into my truck, and with the briefest stop at home to change clothes, I was off to Madaket. I went from behind my desk at the front of a history classroom at 2:20, when the day's final bell rang, to behind the wheel of my skiff in less than an hour, and I had the entire lingering, luxurious June evening before me. Liz, my wife, was heading home from behind her English desk, though perhaps not as quickly, to spend the afternoon and evening with our son, Chick. She would play with him, feed him dinner, and bathe him. Perhaps I would be home in time to put him to bed, though I had been careful not to fully commit. I planned to maximize my fishing time, having somehow amassed enough childcare credits for my wife to allow me an evening on the flats. I had been looking forward to the trip immensely. Driving out Hither Creek, I was filled with nothing but anticipation, but once I started to cast, something was not right.

Never before, in my time on the water, had I felt a vague tug in any other direction, at least not since I quit drinking and shed the constant vague tug toward a bar or a party. The compass of my soul has always pointed to the ocean, the magnetism nowhere stronger than Madaket Harbor in the spring when stripers cruised the shallow flats. Cleaning and chores certainly never beckoned. Television and relaxation were given no consideration, and even the substantial pleasures of literature and food were postponed or skipped entirely without question. I have always been at home on the water, at home chasing fish.

When I am on the flats of Madaket in June, gliding over the eel grass, scanning the surface for waking stripers, or trolling around offshore in July waiting for the scream of a reel, or on the Bonito Bar in August waiting for a jolt be transmitted up my braided line, I am content and fulfilled. Conversely, if I find myself on the couch, in an office, or just about any place on land, I feel I am squandering precious time on inconsequential nonsense. Fishing is panacea.

But last night, for the first time, drifting those sacred Madaket flats, formerly the magnetic north for the compass of my soul, I considered the possibility that I should be, and even perhaps wanted to be, somewhere else. At first, I did not recognize the feeling, and I was just discontent. Then I was irritated and confused, not quite able to pinpoint the cause of my discontentedness. It was a mystery to me, why a clear, warm June evening, on glassy calm flats brimming with stripers was not providing the euphoria I had come to associate with it. Eventually, after a few casts and even a catch and release, I pieced it together. I wanted to see my son and my wife. It had been a long week at school, and I, accustomed to years of finding solace on the ocean, immediately raced to my beloved Madaket flats to find peace and happiness. I had not realized that the compass of my soul now pointed away from the ocean and away from the fish. From now on, it would always point toward my son.

It was a perfect night for fishing, though, and I stayed on the flats and kept casting. As soon as I pinpointed the source of my discontent, missing my son and my wife, I felt better about it. It was a far better alternative than the flats somehow losing their appeal to me, or worse yet, having my placid fishing interrupted by thoughts of bills, career concerns, or other inconsequential nonsense. I could surely accept that my son and my family would occupy my heart and my mind enough to distract me from fishing, whereas the thought of having anything else encroach into fishing would have been intolerable.

The life of any man, or any person for that matter, is changed dramatically upon parenthood; commitments exist to a degree that was previously unimaginable. But these changes can be particularly difficult in the life of a fishing nut. A true fishing nut has already streamlined, shirked, or postponed so many aspects of life that non-anglers would label "priorities," that they can begin to feel their fishing time is impenetrable. Problems, situations, all manner of life issues, have cropped up, and they have fished through it all, and it becomes easy for them to assume nothing will come between them and the water. That is not to say that these fishing nuts plan to or want to be less than totally devoted parents. It is just that they have been able to work out their situations in the past while remaining dedicated anglers, and on some level, they suspect parenting will be another one of those situations. Although I rationally realized that parenting assumed a higher status than angling in my priorities, there existed a little devil on my shoulder wearing Costa Del Mars and holding a fly rod. He whispered to me things like, "Don't worry about it, you'll be able to get out on the water all the time."

In his classic *Trout Bum*, John Gierach writes, "The fact that I'm single now only illustrates that a sportsman of my caliber can't possibly live with someone whose ducks aren't in a row." He makes this statement in regard to spending money on fly

19

tackle that his significant other felt should have been used to fix a leaking roof. While I certainly agree with Gierach's priorities, I am not sure how many others do, particularly significant others, regardless of whether their ducks are in a row or not. I have met very few men (and no women) who place fishing at the top of their priorities, and I think in a lot of practical circumstances, the observation could be shortened to: "The fact that I'm single now only illustrates that a sportsman of my caliber can't possibly live with someone."

By the time I read *Trout Bum*, I was already involved with my wife-to-be, and quite happy about it. I would not have forsaken romance, commitment, and a family for a life more dedicated to sport, but I had a feel for where Gierach's sentiment was coming. For the previous couple of years, I had been doing a pretty good job as a fishing bum myself, though saltwater species, and not trout, were my target. I fished nearly every day from when the stripers arrived in the spring until October. In May and June, many of those trips would be on my own or with friends, and by July they would almost exclusively be with clients. I tried to fish as much as possible in the winter as well, and while I was never quite successful at chasing fish full-time once the fish left Nantucket in the fall, I usually managed to make it south for some fishing.

The winter before meeting Liz, I spent three months running a charter boat in Costa Rica, and that seemed like a good gig. I was paid very little, and the boat was not busy, but I was hanging out in Costa Rica and occasionally being paid to go fishing. I was just starting to figure out some important things, like where to fish for roosterfish without burning too much fuel on days that I did not have charters, when it was time to come back home. I was looking forward to returning the next winter. It was 2008, and just as my summer season was winding down and I was thinking about heading south again, the economy imploded. Nobody was taking costly fishing trips to Costa Rica, and the whole thing fell apart. For my part, having recently met the woman who would become my wife, I did not try very hard to piece it together, because while it was going to be a winter on Nantucket, it did not look like it was going to be a lonely winter on Nantucket.

A few months later a pipe burst in the house she was renting. It caused substantial damage, forcing her to look for a new place. We determined that while it seemed a bit soon in the relationship to start cohabitating, that step was in our future, and given the circumstances, we might as well start now. I was in love and generally thrilled with the entire situation, though I had gone from totally unattached to living together fairly rapidly, while perhaps not realizing the extent to which a significant other would conflict with my aggressive fishing schedule.

In lieu of heading back to Costa Rica, I spent the winter scalloping. The transition from the warm Pacific teeming with sailfish to semi-frozen Nantucket harbor reluctant to surrender shellfish was difficult. As a reward for those months of hard labor in freezing weather, I decided to hop on a plane to Pine Island, FL, and spend the month of April fishing. Scallop season closes March 31st, and stripers don't arrive until late April at the earliest. My schedule was clear, and April is a good time to be fishing in Florida. While my lovely new girlfriend had made a long Nantucket winter warm and pleasant, it was visions of redfish and snook that sustained me through the final weeks of the scallop season.

Liz objected to a month-long fishing sabbatical. The first sign that she didn't "have her ducks in a row". Having met in the fall with fishing all but over, my fishing, in her experience, was all just theoretical, and not being terribly familiar with fishing or fishermen, I suppose she had no idea what to expect. Eventually, I convinced her that the fishing trip was not only a good idea, it was completely necessary for my own mental health. Her objection was also mitigated by the fact that as a high school teacher she has a week off in April, and she would join me for about a week in the middle of the month.

I went fishing, I had a great time, and I caught a lot of fish. She visited, and we had a great time and caught more fish. In the end, it did not cause a significant amount of relationship strife. It was significant only in that it was the first time I encountered any resistance about a fishing trip from somebody other than my mother, and I have been dealing with her resistance for so long that it is no longer noteworthy.

While the trip was made only with the best intentions, I will admit that it also crossed my mind that I was setting a good precedent early in the relationship. If I needed to go fishing, I would go, and it would be something that could be expected with some regularity throughout the course of our lives together. We also loosely agreed upon the policy that fishing trips of less than two weeks required no approval and could be scheduled as time and money allowed, while any excursion longer than two weeks would require a talk and her approval. It will come as no surprise, since I am now happily married with a child, that this policy has been thrown out the window and I now require permission for even the briefest local fishing trip, never mind one that involves travel. With the family also came the need and desire for a job more stable than a fishing guide and a scalloper, and the last couple springs have found me in a classroom working as a teacher, further limiting my time on the water.

While it was once rare for me to miss a day on the flats in June, for the past two seasons I have probably averaged two or three trips a week. Having your fishing trips cut by sixty percent is tough to take, but looked at from a different point of view, that of having a small child, a wife, and a job, still being able to go fishing two or three times a week puts me in a very enviable situation.

I think there is a decent chance that I will not be fully able to recoup my fishing time for about twenty years. I anticipate that by that time my childcare responsibilities will consist mostly of writing large checks, and while I may still want to supervise my son directly, he will probably not stand for it. As for my wife, I expect that in twenty years she will either have become a devout angler herself and we will fish together or she will have tired of my company and want me out of the house as much as possible.

However, there are some positive signs about my fishing future within those twenty years. My Uncle Bob, a pretty devoted fishing bum in his own right for a while, has twin daughters who are now eight. My years of tremendous fishing freedom coincided with his years of tremendous parental responsibility. For years he had to field several weekly calls from me asking if he was able to get out fishing. The answer was almost uniformly no, to the point where I felt bad calling to inform him that I would once again be fishing while he was unable to, but I couldn't stop calling because there existed the very occasional yes. Not offering when he would have actually been able to go would have been far worse than dangling any number of trips he was unable to go on in front of his eyes. The encouraging sign is that it seems that for about the past year when I call to see if he can go fishing, the answer is yes more than no. Although the fact that I now call once or twice a week to see about a fishing trip, rather than five or six times, may have something to do with the greater proportion of yeses. Even more encouraging is the fact that his daughters now fish. Certainly, taking my son Chick fishing is one of the things I look forward to most, and I imagine that my fishing time will increase drastically when I am able to take Chick off his mother's hands for a while.

In America today, childcare as predominantly the responsibility of mothers is an anachronism. In every parenting relationship I am familiar with, including my own, the parents keep a sort of running tally on who is owed personal time. I do not know anybody who actually writes it down, but in a few cases this is not done magnanimously; it is because both Mom and Dad feel they can use the lack of a written record to skew the numbers in their favor. If Mom gets to go out with the girls Friday night, Dad gets to golf Sunday morning, and if Dad puts the kids to bed, then Mom takes them to the playground, etc. Most of my friends actively suggest and encourage their wives to take weekends away, not because they truly feel their wife could use a spa weekend, but because they will be "owed" a reciprocal fishing trip.

In my case, any fishing that isn't with a client gets placed firmly and precisely on my side of the personal time ledger. To be fair, my wife is usually not very concerned with the ledger, actually cherishing time spent with our son, and she is pretty flexible, especially during fishing season when a strict accounting would probably not come out in my favor. Regardless, as soon as Chick is old enough to come with me, as long as he likes it, I am all set. Then I can take him fishing and it will count toward Mom's off-time, and it is only fair that she return the favor and give me some off time, during which I could go fishing. I could take Chick fishing two or three times a week, and then fish another two or three days a week while his mother is returning the favor. In that manner, I could recoup a vast amount of my fishing time, but to anticipate it coming close to the kind of fishing time I enjoyed as a partially-employed, unattached twenty-something is probably foolhardy. Remember that I once had permission to schedule fishing trips of less than two weeks at will.

At some point after I read Gierach's passage, I was at a party and a friend of mine was telling a story. He said he was leaving in a few days to going fishing in Alaska. He had a friend who had moved there to fish, and as he told it, "he quit his job, sold his house, divorced his wife, and that was that." His tone and delivery suggested that divorcing his wife was just as necessary for his relocation to Alaska as quitting his job. I got a kick out of the story; my wife did not.

The fact that there are people out there who have avoided or shaken off familial ties in order to continue unimpeded with their outdoor habits is no surprise, but that is not for me. When I back my boat into the slip, having somebody on the dock smiling and waving is the perfect ending. After a chilly spring evening chasing stripers, it is nice to crawl under the covers to a warm and sweet smelling spouse. Fishing is something, and love is something else, and I am unwilling to go without either. Then of course there is Chick, and being a parent is an experience I was never willing to give up, not for all the fish in the world.

In addition to all the sentimental stuff and the fact they make life worthwhile, having a family also seems practical in terms of leading a well-balanced life. Being a renaissance man appeals to me. I enjoy cooking, reading, and racquet sports. I dabble amateurishly in woodworking. At some point I would like to take up watercolors. I ordered a watercolor kit over the internet, but when it arrived my wife declared (very convincingly) that I did not need another expensive, unprofitable, time-consuming, selfish pursuit. To her chagrin, my mother-in-law also got me a watercolor kit for Christmas, but for the time being both are packed away in my basement.

When you are a fishing nut, you run the risk of most of life's events falling into two categories: "fishing" and "unimportant stuff in between fishing". I lived pretty close to this for a little while, and my life quickly takes on that flavor again when my wife is gone. Extreme hours are kept, meals are take-out or skipped, the house is not cleaned, the only thing I read is a tide chart, and most waking moments are spent in the pursuit of fish. It is nice for a little while, but I am not sure it is any way to live. Like Gus Orviston's ideal schedule in *The River Why*, it begins to wear on you quicker than you think. You spend a good chunk of your life wanting nothing more than to be able to fish all the time, but after a few weeks or even a few days of fishing all the time, it can get old. Not only are life's pleasures outside of fishing ignored, but the fishing can become less pleasurable too.

Variety is the spice of life. In that very practical regard, it is important either to have a family or take up watercolors, or perhaps some day in my case, both.

The issue in my life was never how to avoid encumbrances or commitments. I always wanted a spouse and a family to love and to share my life with, and while I may have underestimated the amount they would cut into my fishing time, no amount of time would be too costly. The issue has become how to balance family and fishing, or rather, how to keep as much fishing as possible in my life while still being the kind of husband and father I want to be. If variety is the spice of life, than fishing is the main ingredient, and I am a man who likes big portions.

It is easy, very easy, to lapse into thinking the grass is always greener. When I am changing a diaper or at a playground, it is easy to remember the days of changing flies and floating around on the flats all day and to wish I was there, forgetting that in between fish on the flats, it was equally easy to think about the possibility of true love or what it may be like to have a child. It is important to remember the bad with the good, if only momentarily, for the purpose of realizing how good things currently are. I loved living in Costa Rica, I loved the freedom, I loved the wild beauty of the place. Living in a place a little less tame and a little more frontier than the United States was thrilling, and I certainly loved the fishing, but I was lonely. It is easy now to fantasize about being back, but life there was not perfect. When I was there I longed for companionship, now I have it beyond my aspirations; to lament the freedom I gave up to get it is silly. Many of my dreams have come true, I have a smart, beautiful, compassionate wife who makes me laugh and a happy, healthy son.

My life these days is not a search for balance, because balance suggests a search for equality, and nothing will equal Chick and Liz. My life is a desperate search for more hours in the day. My life is shaped by the attempt to negotiate competing demands on time, making my wife happy, caring for my son, and keeping my own sanity by fishing, and for the first time in my life, by not fishing. It has shaped my life for the past couple years and will continue to shape it for the foreseeable future. Sometimes it is difficult, often it is absurd, sometimes it is sad, often fulfilling, and sometimes unrewarding, but mostly it is wonderful.

3

Fly Fishing as a Path to Tolerance

My wife is in the second stage of planning my son's second birthday party. The first stage began hours after he was born. A working outline of birthday parties for ages one through twelve was in place before we left the hospital. The first stage, the planning stage, continues basically non-stop around the calendar year, interrupted only by the actual execution of a party, at the conclusion of which, the party is reviewed in detail with an eye toward what can be executed better next year. His second birthday is in a few weeks, and we are nearing the end of the second stage (I sincerely hope), which is defined by the accumulation of supplies. A week or so before the party we will enter the last stage which is total party submersion. Conversation or activity unrelated to party preparation is forbidden, and there will be a fairly high level of hysteria.

A few months before his first birthday, we were invited to another first birthday. There were kids from six months to sixteen years running wild all over the place. There were lots of toys, snacks, screaming, crying, diapers (clean and otherwise), and bewildered parents. Parents with children too young to be left to their own devices tried to navigate the rooms following their children, and spent the entirety of party with the fear that one or more of the adults had drank just enough Heinekens to step on a child. There was a tremendous amount of scolding. Dads got scolded for drinking Heinekens while mothers followed crawling babies and toddling toddlers, mothers were scolded for forgetting diapers, grandfathers scolded for eating too much potato salad, and children scolded for bonking other children, stealing toys, and stealing Heinekens.

The whole scene was nightmarish, and when we left, my wife agreed that Chick's first birthday would be a sedate, intimate affair. I agreed, strongly, citing that in truth, we should reward ourselves. We deserved to be rewarded for making it through a year of parenting. Chick, at the age of one, would have no idea it was his birthday anyway, and I felt it would be fitting for him to spend the night with his grandparents while his mother and I relaxed at a restaurant after a tiresome year. While she refused to go that far, she was onboard with a sedate, intimate affair.

And then she wasn't. The party grew, as Hemingway wrote, "In two ways. Gradually, then suddenly." First the guest list expanded beyond the grandparents. Friends were included, and then to avoid the impossible task of choosing which friends, more friends were added. You can't invite friends and exclude family. Our house as the venue became too small and it was moved to my parents. They invited friends. Gear was ordered, my wife started Googling and Pinteresting *"Sesame Street* parties" and any restraint or moderation still clinging to the affair was swept away.

My wife suggested live goldfish to be given as party favors, and I laughed. Her sense of humor is superb, and I assumed the goldfish routine was a little spoof of herself. As the party snowballed out of control, there had been some conversations in which differences of opinion were aired, and while I had long since given up trying to control the size and scope of the affair, it was no secret that I was not thrilled with the way things were going. Live goldfish were so ridiculous it could only be a joke, and not an unfunny one. My wife did not laugh and though it took some convincing, she made me believe she was serious. The theme of the party was *Sesame Street*; apparently Elmo has a pet goldfish, and I was informed that live goldfish were a necessity at any decent *Sesame Street* party.

I had an ironclad two-pronged argument against live goldfish. First, bestowing a live pet on children without prior approval from their parents is outrageous. The parents will be forced either to care for it, to arrange an adoption, turn it loose, or murder it, and that is not an appealing choice you want to force on your friends. And since Chick was one, we told him who his friends were, and they were the children of *our* friends.

Second, and an even stronger argument than not wanting to infuriate all of our friends, was that there is not a pet store on Nantucket. It would not be easy to infuriate our friends; we would need to import the goldfish to do it. The main attribute of the goldfish as a party favor, over say, a kitten, was that the commitment on behalf of the parents was in all likelihood a short-term one. But, when trying to import them, their propensity for dying was a distinct disadvantage. I told Liz I anticipated a high mortality rate during the flight or boat ride to the island and the ensuing wait. She agreed to no goldfish, perhaps knowing her point was not a winner and therefore unwilling to argue it, or perhaps she agreed in good faith only to change her position later. A few days later, without any further discussion (argument), I was informed that goldfish bowls emblazoned with the names of Chick's guests had been special-ordered and my mother-in-law, in addition to many, many additional party supplies, would be traveling to the island with dozens of live goldfish. Liz had informed the parents of the party guests, and none had strong objections. In defeat and still anticipating high mortality, I suggested a couple more dozen.

In the end, the party was truly a success. Our friends came, family came, and we all enjoyed some time together. For his part, Chick seemed to enjoy the decorations and snacks and everything else that his Mom had taken great care in, and the children who were slightly older seemed to enjoy all that stuff even more. There were not even any goldfish fatalities in-transit, though they started dropping like flies in the days following the party. We even made a covert delivery of a couple spare fish to our friend's house because their child had not yet become bored with the goldfish, and its demise was deemed too quick. Luckily, we had extras and were happy to be unburdened (ironically, Liz had absolutely no desire for a pet goldfish).

As an angler, and perhaps to an even greater degree as a fly fisherman, it is hard to pass judgment on the practicality of how others spend their time and money. Perhaps no reasonable person would throw an over the top gala complete with live goldfish party favors for their son's first birthday. If I had my way, the time and resources would be diverted toward fishing. The time I spent fulfilling my wife's lengthy party related to-do lists (despite repeated assurances that my own responsibilities would be minimal) would have been better spent tying flies, organizing tackle boxes and bags, or rigging lures. The money spent on invitations, decorations, favors, custom-made birthday shirts, and personalized goldfish bowls was better spent on a new rod, a new reel, a plane ticket south, or saved for a boat.

By this I do not mean to usurp funds allocated to my son, though how much of the party was for him and how much of it was for his mother is certainly debatable. Regardless, the idea is for him to derive the most benefit from the time and money, and I believe the benefits of future fishing would substantially outweigh the benefits of providing his friends with customized goldfish bowls. Skimping on his birthday just to add to his college fund may be practical, but it is also lame. Perhaps in addition to his college fund, I could start a boat fund for him.

Forgo the fancy birthday party and about half of the gifts and put that money into a boat fund, and sometime in his late teens or early twenties he could buy a boat. It is a good age to have a boat and a bad age to be able to afford one. Twenty-somethings with boats can spend a lot of time floating around the ocean trying to figure out what to do with themselves as adults, while twenty-somethings without boats may try to figure that out in bars or worse.

Of course, he would probably be able to borrow my boat at that age, but having his own may be beneficial. If it is low on gas, he will need to fill it, and if it breaks, he will have to fix it. At the same time, if he wants to trailer it to the Keys, I will be in a position to say nothing more than "good luck" and perhaps, "when can I fly down to fish with you?" It is a good age to get some real experience with both responsibility and freedom.

Whether the funds are set aside for future boats, spent on reels and plane tickets, or even donated in Chick's name to the Billfish Foundation, Stripers Forever, or some other organization fighting for his fishing future, anything would be an improvement.

During the preparation for Chick's second birthday, as I saw the guest list grow, and as I saw gear accumulate and paychecks disappear, my objections once again came to mind. My fly tying desk was overtaken with poster board, cardboard, glue, and little party hats. I was told to use the materials to build Mickey Mouse hats for the guests. I pondered why both my time and space were being usurped by this unreasonable nonsense. To what end is this? I thought of all the fishing-related things I could be doing. Then I thought, to what end is my fishing? At first, I contemplated the question as a means toward building another logical argument with which to assail the size and scope the second birthday currently taking over my life. But, over time, it occurred to me that my own predilection to devote every

33

available resource toward fishing might not be universally judged as inherently reasonable.

I do not even know where to start reflecting on my own fishing because there is so much of it, and there is scarcely a corner of my life that fishing does not spill into somehow. But for the sake of starting the reflection somewhere, lets start with a low-key local trip. A favorite local trip of mine is to Madaket Harbor and the flats of Tuckernuck. Not a fantastic commitment of time, it is even possible to pop out and back in two or three hours. Not a fantastic commitment of money either, perhaps a couple hundred bucks in tackle amortized over many fishing trips and just a couple bucks in gas. And perhaps it remains that way for some folks, maybe even quite a few folks, but that is not the case with me. The trip snowballs, not unlike my wife's party planning. For tackle, I will probably need, at the very least, a spinning rod and a fly rod. It is possible and even likely that I will use one exclusively for the entire trip, but while I see the virtue in travelling light, I tend to lean toward the "better to have it and not need it than need it and not have it" school of thought. On a trip to those waters I will probably be using a Hogy or another soft plastic bait, but it is possible I will want to switch to a Mirrolure or another walk-the-dog type lure, and then I may even want to switch back. Of course I could just tie them on as I wanted, but why do that when I could just bring another rod? Also, the light rod that flings the soft plastic nicely seems a little on the flimsy side for casting the lure, so I will need to purchase a couple specialized rods. Never mind the half-dozen I have in the shed already; they are all either six inches too short or long or rated for five-pound test too many. The line was once fairly negligible, but not anymore. The reels must be filled with Spectra braid to the tune of about thirty bucks a spool and add a piece of fluorocarbon from another pricey spool to the end of that.

Next is the fly tackle, a marketplace in which many of the prices seem to be based on satire. My own rod is a modest one at less than $300 (and I only have about four of them), but I like the gold colored reels with the engraved nameplate on the side that says "Matt Reinemo" (and they cost significantly more than a similarly engraved goldfish bowl). Additionally, my friend Jake recently turned me on to some very snazzy fly reels by Cheeky, and I can not imagine going any length of time without picking up a few of those. Just a fly line these days will run you close to a hundred bucks, and a leader, assembled from more spools of pricy fluorocarbon must be attached to the end of that. And like many fly fisherman I know, I need to spend a couple hundred (read thousand) on specialized vices, a wide array of tools, and bags, boxes, bunches and piles of feathers, furs, hairs, tinsels, eyes, threads, epoxies and hooks. Money foolishly spent to try and save money on flies, but well spent as art supplies.

All this, if you recall, is for a brief local trip to the flats. Add another batch of tackle for rip fishing, and another for bonito and false albacore. Finally, there is offshore fishing and for the price of those rods, reels, lines and lures you could buy a decent car. The mere mention of fuel bills and boat ownership moves any discussion of money into the absurd. The fantastic devotion of financial resources is not even the whole picture. In fact, it is merely the beginning.

For starters, the large and expensive collection of fly tying materials needs to be lovingly assembled into flies, and I will tie flies in spurts all winter, as time allows. Sometimes it is actually pretty good family time: I sit at my desk and tie, and talk with Liz while Chick plays with his toys or watches cartoons. Nevertheless, it is time spent on fishing, with no off-season. While I try to get all my tying done from November through April, rather than banging out a few dozen each of known producers I am always partial to trying to invent the next great fly, or trying a new method, or hybridizing and amending accepted patterns. As a result my box is largely comprised of pairs and prototypes. When one proves effective, I am left scrambling back to the vise in the midst of the fishing season to spin up a half-dozen replicas. I have gotten better at this over the past couple seasons, knowing I will need several deceivers for the flats, several chunky sand eels for Great Point, and many, many bonito bunny variations for bonito and false albacore. Regardless of my needs, sitting at the vise, dreaming, thinking and creating remains more appealing to me than the rote assembly of a dozen bonito bunnies.

In addition to the flies tied for Nantucket, if any fishing travel is on the horizon (which it is as often as possible, and another significant category of expenses I left out above), I will usually spend quite a while tying new flies for the intended species and destination. It is also likely that the new flies will require a new influx of hooks, eyes, furs, and hairs. In addition to my home flies, I currently have a serious box (a Cliff's Bugger Beast) devoted to bonefish and permit and another box of what I refer to as "assorted Southern flies".

I struggle with neatness and organization, and fly tying generally leaves my desk littered with all manner of supplies. After a few sessions, I am forced to clean it, either at my wife's insistence or because my tools have vanished into the unruly piles of bucktails and synthetic hair. I would like to classify this as time spent on "cleaning," perhaps Liz's favorite way for me to spend my time, as opposed to time spent on "fishing stuff." Liz's prioritization of "fishing stuff" correlates with my prioritization on party planning for infants. After the fly tying and the cleaning, there is the organization and rigging of spinning tackle. This will take place in two major sessions, at the beginning and end of each season, augmented by several minor sessions throughout the year. Any travel involving fishing usually requires its own medium-sized organization.

Incidental fishing time may include shopping for fishing stuff, dreaming of and/or shopping for fishing trips, working on or shopping for sportfishing artwork, or reading about fishing. I do about ninety percent of my non-fiction reading and a chunk of my fiction reading on fishing, and I am a serious reader, so that time is not insignificant.

This is all on top of actually *going* fishing, and I assure you this is not one of those situations in which more time is spent in preparation than on the actual event. In my mid-twenties I once left my mother a note in late April that said, "Stripers are here, I have gone fishing. See you in October. Love, Matt." It was facetious of course, but closer to the truth than you might imagine and always sort of a working goal. Certainly, my commitments and expectations have changed in the intervening years, but the memory of that note is still with me. It still serves some purpose, still stands for something, and still functions as a kind of lunatic mission statement.

After this reflection, it is not lost on me that Liz could throw catered, black tie birthday parties at upscale venues with multiple live acts for a fraction of the time and money I spend on fishing.

We, as anglers, know of course that this tremendous expenditure of time and resources is toward the loftiest of goals. Time in nature observing and admiring the natural world is a noble pursuit on its own. Add to that the wondrous element of trying to outwit predators who are inextricably woven into that natural world, a world that as humans we seem to isolate ourselves from more all the time. It is a fantastic pursuit of the elusive, a quest worthy of lifetime devotion and then some. It is the path to a vivacious enlightenment; no price could be too high, and no amount of time could be considered excessive.

But put another way, every year I spend countless hours and thousands of dollars in pursuit of fish, which when I catch, I usually immediately let go, with no apparent change in me or the fish. When it is put that way, personalized goldfish bowls seem a modest indulgence.

Faced with this information, I could stand my ground. I could argue until my last breath that the time and money spent on fishing is irreplaceable, that it is worthwhile, that it is important, that it is a path to contentment and a higher consciousness, and it is fun. I could also cling to the belief that my wife's birthday celebrations for our son have been overly extravagant and recklessly expensive and wasteful bacchanalias of consumerism. I could even do all of the above believing I was right.

But it is an argument I will no longer make, a stand I will not take. After some more careful consideration, I wonder if Liz takes away some kind of happiness and some kind of satisfaction from the parties, perhaps an indescribable satisfaction akin in some way to my own satisfaction from fishing. To take it is a step farther, maybe a particular satisfaction is to be had from a well-planned, heavily festooned, grand party. Catching a striper on any tackle makes me happy, but one caught on a fly rod with a fly I lovingly assembled leads to greater joy. Perhaps a cake, a few friends, and some smiles from our son would make Liz happy, but pure, googley-eyed wonderment from our son and all the guests leads to a deep personal satisfaction.

When you have made it your life's work to catch fish in order to let them go, and you go about it one by one preferring the inefficient, albeit artistic, method of fly fishing, it lends itself well to taking an extremely tolerant view toward how others decide to spend their time and money.

Liz will get no more argument from me on the frivolity of birthday parties, nor will anybody wanting to devote all their available resources to model trains, sailing a boat around on the wind, hitting a little white ball over large distances into a small hole, getting pretty flowers to grow, recreating Civil War battles or planning extravagant parties. Instead, I will say have fun, good luck, and may it do for you some small fraction of what fishing does for me. After all, they could squander all their time on stuff like careers, religion, and politics.

4

Tales of Jealousy and Marlin

On television, in articles, and in advertisements, fishing guides often say things like, "I just love the excitement of people catching fish," or "watching my customers catch fish is more fun than doing it myself," or some other pleasant statement about their demeanor and their thoughts on their customers and guests catching fish while they catch nothing. It causes me to wonder if I am missing this magnanimous fishing guide gene; maybe I have been lucky to squeak by without it. Are these guys really just as happy when somebody else is doing the catching, or are they putting on an act for the camera trying to seem nice and attract business? I think for the most part, they are full of shit, and if given the opportunity, they sure as hell would prefer to just catch fish themselves. If they truly derived all the satisfaction and fulfillment from customers catching fish that they claimed, they would probably spend their days-off on land, getting to know the wife and kids again, running errands, or in some other pursuit, but that is hardly the case. Among the decent fishing guides I know, a day off from guiding in the season seldom means a day off from fishing. They are, on average, more eager to grab a rod than any two clients.

This is not to say that I do not enjoy customers catching fish, I do. It sure as hell beats customers *not* catching fish. Certainly if children are involved, engaged, and excited, that can make for a truly special time. However, a summer day seldom passes when my longtime mate and fishing nut buddy Mike Schuster and I do not plan, speculate, or dream about our next trip sans customers. Mike is generally concerned with the size of his bank account and he occasionally inquires about future bookings, marketing, expansion or some other business concern. I consistently reply that my personal business plan is to eventually eliminate all the customers, freeing up my schedule to fish on my own. Of course, I have never acted on this and all my actions in building a guide business have been to the contrary, but my parents would nevertheless use the statement against me as evidence of misguided priorities illustrative of something wrong with me.

Sometimes, instead of excitement or generosity or any other positive sentiment, the feeling I have toward customers is plain envy. It is not with every fish, or even every big fish, but once in a while it just strikes me that I would like to be on the business end of a rod instead of poling, driving the boat or offering advice. Watching somebody else catch a fish you wanted is an experience sure to bring on feelings of jealousy. When they catch the fish due to your guiding, experience and knowledge, as well as, to varying degrees, your mutual good luck, it can cast the experience in a number of interesting lights.

First, if the customer is a total dope, and wholly undeserving of catching the fish, it is generally no fun at all. This sentiment has already been identified and explored in some wonderful literature. In Norman Maclean's *A River Runs Through It*, Norman says of his father, "If our father had had his say, nobody who did not know how to catch a fish would be allowed to disgrace a fish by catching him." Occasionally, it seems I am in the business of disgracing fish.

On such occasions I have the urge to unhook the fish, drop it back over the side and offer an apology along the lines of I'm very sorry sir, I won't bother you again, or at least not until I am back with somebody worthy, or on my own. The fictitious young Tom Skelton, in Tom McGuane's *Ninety-Two in the Shade*, becomes the hero to all fishing guides who have felt this way when the undeserving client, Rudleigh, hooks a permit and Skelton tracks it back through a mangrove channel only to unhook it and let it go. I have never done such a thing, and certainly, losing a client's fish on purpose is one of least professional things a guide can do, but I would be lying if I said the idea hadn't crossed my mind.

In my second year running the *Topspin*, a customer caught a fifty-inch, forty-pound striper that to this day remains the biggest striper I have caught, or at least weighed. Since then I have caught two others that were forty-eight inches that probably weighed as much or more than that somewhat slender fish, but I was "bluefishing" at rips beyond three miles both times and the fish were released. The customer who caught the fifty-incher was a very nice woman, supremely ignorant of the angling feat she had just accomplished. She was vacationing on Nantucket enjoying a half-day fishing with her father (who had already caught a forty-three-incher and was also unaccustomed to fishing), and was polite and mildly pleased with her fish, which was her first striper. She remained totally unaware of the extent any true striper angler would have gone to in order to catch a fifty-inch fish. I was thrilled to have such a wonderful fish onboard, in quite a bit of awe as to just how monstrous the thing looked, and looking forward to the photos, hoopla, and celebration that would ensue at the dock upon bringing in such a fish. My mate and I tried to impart to her some degree of appreciation commensurate with this fish of a lifetime, and while she remained cheerful and polite, I got the feeling she was perplexed as to what all the fuss was about. I was jealous, my mate was jealous, past and present customers were jealous, and certainly it seemed a crime against striper devotees everywhere that such a fish would fall to such an angler, when in all likelihood, she would have enjoyed herself even more had there been some cooperative bluefish around because they jump when they fight.

On an interesting and related note, and an example of no good deed going unpunished, I deserved to find that fish as a second-year nineteen-year old charter captain about as much as my novice angler deserved to reel it in. The truth is, I was having a slow day, not having much success finding fish anywhere. Josh Eldridge on his *Monomoy*, at the time a 31' Bertram, had found the fish off Wauwinet and happily had them to himself. After I expressed some woes on the radio, he took pity on me and called me over only to have me arrive and pull out that behemoth. I am not sure if Josh was jealous at all, but if the situation was reversed and I had called him over, I suspect I would have flown into a blind rage.

Upon a remarkable catch by a client there are usually mixed feelings. Genuine happiness for your client, your mutual good fortune, perhaps some professional satisfaction for a job well done, accompanied by a passing thought that you sure would like to throw a lure or a fly to these biting fish, or the realization that the striper your client is holding up is bigger than any you've caught this season. This is probably the feeling most familiar to those accustomed to fishing with their friends. You honestly want your fishing buddies to have a good time, you want them to catch fish, and you wish them no ill will. You do not regard them as disgracing every fish they catch, and if you are to play a role in the success, i.e. driving the boat, netting, leadering or gaffing, you are focused and determined. However, you would also like to out-fish your buddy and their successes; while joyous, are not entirely free of envy.

Finally, at the other end of the spectrum, is feeling totally happy, selfless and comfortable not being the one catching the fish. If a fishing genie popped out of your tackle box, and said you could switch places and be the angler with no consequences whatsoever, you would reply, nope, I'm alright here. Your joy and exuberance with the fight and the catch is equal, or perhaps greater than, if you had done it yourself. Interestingly enough, the first example of this that comes to mind is a magnificent catch that I am desperate to duplicate and have never accomplished as an angler. In August of 2012, Bill Palmer caught and released a white marlin onboard *Topspin* with Mike and me. And given the chance to rewrite history and be the angler, I would leave things just the way they went.

If Mike had caught it, I would be pissed. If Liz had been on the boat, I would not have let her touch the rod. If anybody else had caught it, there would have been envy, but to have Bill on the rod was pure joy. A lot of things need to be just right for this to be the case. First, the angler needs to be experienced enough to be deserving, yet not so experienced as to lessen the accomplishment. The friendship and history that Bill and I share is perhaps the most important factor in my lack of envy.

Bill started fishing with me when I was nineteen, in my second year of running the boat. He was a skilled and experienced fishermen on a family vacation, happy to spend a half day with them on the water. Those were the years when schools of big stripers were fairly common along the Wauwinet shoreline between Great Point and Sankaty, and we spent our first trips together there, catching big bass on wire line. Over time, we moved away from the wire line because we both preferred lighter tackle, and away from striped bass as their population, and hence availability in August, dwindled. We started to spend a lot of time on the Bonito Bar, and instead of one fishing trip over the course of his vacation, we would do three or five. We fished offshore, east of the island when little

45

bluefin were prevalent, and we went south and shark fished, almost always successful at finding makos. For more than a decade we chased most fish that Nantucket had to offer, and over that time, became pretty close friends without ever trying. Bill had spent plenty of time offshore in the Northeast before ever meeting me, and between his remembrances and my own fixation, white marlin were often discussed and never far from our minds, especially when we were shark fishing in what was once some very productive white marlin water.

When Bill came to Nantucket in 2011, there were some fairly consistent reports of white marlin, for the first time in a long time. It had become Bill's habit to come down and visit me on the dock on the day he arrived, to say hello, catch up a bit and nail down the details of our fishing plans, which more often than not commenced the next day. When he strolled up, we said hello and I became fidgety. I just about whispered, "there are white marlin down there." I may have feared that the marlin might overhear me from the dock. If they were capable of disappearing for a more than a decade, they may also be cunning and fickle enough to hear me plotting on the dock and take off to the mid-Atlantic, the Azores, or parts unknown. Or perhaps it was just such a long shot that I felt even mentioning the fish at full volume was outrageous. It was more like I was telling him where I thought we could score drugs than what fish we may find. Immediately sensing and sharing my sentiments, that these white marlin need to addressed with caution and in hushed tones, he whispered back, "oh yea," and immediately, he got a crazy glint in his eye. In further hushed tones, we planned a shark fishing trip. It was a shark fishing trip on its face because only a fool would plan a trip for a species that hadn't been successfully targeted out of Nantucket in a decade. But Bill and I knew it was really a marlin expedition, and the shark fishing was just a cover, after all, these fish were too savvy to succumb to a straightforward pursuit.

We headed south, with chum and wire leaders for the sharks, but also with a few ballyhoo and live scup in case of marlin. We saw two white marlin. One vanished only a moment after we saw it, and on the next we had a bait in the water in its proximity very quickly, but it showed no interest and we never saw it again. We ended up having a great day, catching a mako and some dolphin from around lobster pots, but it was the marlin that had captured our attention.

When we got back to the dock, we discussed our future plans.

"What do you want to do tomorrow?" Bill asked.

"You know what I want to do," I said, "I want to go south and troll for marlin all day."

"Good, that's what I want to do too," he said, and the next day we embarked on the first marlin fishing charter to leave Straight Wharf in over a decade. We were going to troll all day, and be ready to cast a bait to any marlin we saw tailing. We headed south and spent the morning trolling around where we had found the marlin, the mako, and the bait the day before. After a fruitless hour or so, in what overnight had become a lifeless little patch of water, we picked up our lines and started cruising southwest, looking for signs of fish. We didn't cruise for long before I saw some bait showering. I yelled down to put out the lines. Mike and Bill hustled to get the lines in the water as I swung by the showering bait ball. By the time they had two lines in the water, a marlin was up on one of them. We pitched him a ballyhoo rigged with a circle hook, he ate it, we dropped back to him and then engaged the reel's drag. The rod bent, line screamed and we screamed. On the fish's second sprawling leap, the hook shot back at us, never having made its way into the fish's jaw. We were devastated, but we got right back on the troll. At the time I thought we were going to raise another, but we never did. As the day wore on, I was left contemplating the fact that we had hooked and lost a fish that I had been awaiting

47

for thirteen years, with no idea when the next would appear. The day ended, and then the summer ended, without another marlin encounter.

When Bill arrived the next summer, 2012, tuna fishing east of island was excellent and Mike and I were on a particular hot streak, coming off thirteen fish in eighteen bites over three days of fishing. However, in addition to the hot tuna bite, the Nantucket Shark Tournament had just taken place, and more than one boat in the tournament had seen white marlin. Common sense would have sent us back East, and Mike and my father both wondered out loud about the prudence of heading south on a long odds marlin adventure in the midst of a good tuna bite to the east. But for Bill and me, a rumor of marlin was enough, and I concluded that it was only logical to push the hot streak to the absolute limit, test it and see if a little of the good offshore mojo we had to the east would follow us south. After all, in the long run what difference would catching a few more tuna make? A white marlin was the fish of our dreams.

We headed south and did a long loop around several offshore spots with recent marlin rumors. It was a long morning of looking and not seeing much, but around eleven in the morning we started seeing sickle tails quivering along the surface. We baited one who showed no interest, then another. We tried ballyhoo, we tried scup, and we tried live eels. We trolled around tails, eliciting no interest whatsoever. We baited a pair of marlin we found swimming together, and they both ignored our baits equally. Getting a marlin to casually examine our bait seemed to be the best we could hope for, while some marlin, when presented with a bait, seemed to exhibit pure disdain. Our patience and sanity were pushed to the brink as our fishing time dwindled. It was time to head home, but there were so many marlin around that I was confident we would find another fish. As we motored along, I saw a tail and swung around in front of it. Bill pitched a live eel into its path, and the tail disappeared. It appeared the fish had taken an interest in the eel and had begun pursuit, but after a long day witnessing the maddening dietary restraint of white marlin, we were none too confident. We pessimistically wondered if the marlin had frightened at the sight of the eel and scurried away hastily into the depths.

The three of us stood along the transom intently watching the water, but no longer seeing the tail or any sign of the eel. Bill stood in the middle with the spinning rod in his hands, the bail open. Shivers traveled up the braided line.

"I think he is eating it," Bill said.

"Alright," I said, still not quite ready to believe it.

"I think he ate it, I think he has it," Bill said.

"Is he taking it?" I asked.

"Yes, I think he is taking it." Line was pouring off the spool at an encouraging rate, all of us captivated and hopeful, but still wondering if a scared eel could swim fast enough to pull line off that quickly.

After one of those fishing eternities that lasts a few seconds I said, "Well, let's see if he is there."

"You want me to flip the bail?" Bill asked.

"Yes, flip it, then reel tight to him," I said, and we all held our breath, brimming with unadulterated hope.

Bill flipped the bail, but never had to reel. The rod bent steadily over, and this time, the circle hook found its way to the corner of the marlin's jaw. Line started screaming off the reel. I ran back to the controls and started backing toward the fish. We had hooked another one. We had a solid hook-up and a real chance at a marlin, and I whooped in celebration. At the same time, I overflowed with the special terror of big game fishing that comes from knowing the excruciatingly tenuous nature of your connection to a creature with remarkable speed and power. I wondered if every knot was perfect, if the drag was set properly and if it would remain smooth, if the fluorocarbon would chafe on the fish's bill, if some previously undetected fray in the braid or nick in the leader would betray us now. These sentiments and more caused me to yell at Mike.

Captains yelling at mates is a fundamental and colorful part of big game and charter fishing, though I think Mike would agree that I am normally pretty placid. Verbal assaults are not really my style, and if I am truly dissatisfied with the way things are going, I will usually be silent and just try to do everything myself. We have fished together long enough now that if I do not talk enough he checks in with me to make sure I am not angry with him. I am usually quick enough to talk or joke, or hassle him in some good natured way. Any yelling that I do is not out of anger, it is out of pure, unadulterated excitement.

When it was time for me to get married, in lieu of a traditional bachelor party with booze, drugs, and women of ill repute, I wanted to catch billfish. When I worked in Costa Rica, among the many things I learned was that John Brennan was the best captain in the country, and that if I returned as a customer, he was the guy I wanted to fish with. So for my bachelor party I headed back to Costa Rica with my brother and three friends for three days of fishing with John. We fished on two boats, the second boat run by a captain named Keith. I fished with Keith one of the days and in the course of conversation he told me that the only time he allows himself to swear at the mate (or occasionally a customer) is when a marlin is on or in the spread. That struck me as a very reasonable rule, one that captains, mates and customers could all embrace. If tension, emotion and tempers aren't running high and flying around a little bit when a marlin is involved, then maybe we are in the wrong sport. In the little portion of the Pacific off Golfito that we were fishing, they average about a marlin every three days. I was averaging one a year, and about two a decade, so I figured the rule was even more acceptable as applied to me.

As the marlin swam intently about forty yards in back of the boat, I expressed my thoughts that Mike needed to touch the fucking leader to make it an official catch. Mike had a camera in his hands, hoping to get some shots of the jumping fish, and he felt that my demand for him to touch the leader was about thirty-eight yards premature. I disagreed, told him to put down the goddamn camera, put on his gloves, and I believe I said, "literally sell your fucking soul to touch that leader". He reluctantly agreed and put on his gloves, and shortly thereafter, the fish put on a spectacular aerial display that Mike no doubt would have been able to capture, had he not put down the camera. About thirty-five excruciating yards later, as the not entirely beaten marlin raced from one side of the stern to the other with the leader just out of reach, I decreed that Mike was too short, and that we needed to switch. Perhaps a silly, last minute audible born more from panic than prudence, but it worked. Mike assumed the controls, and I went to the stern, and with my extended reach, I grabbed the leader, bringing our quest to a successful completion. I pulled the leader up, and reached down touching the marlin's bill briefly, and it exploded airborne, popped the leader, and was off. We missed out on the pictures and had only a moment of boatside admiration, but a catch nonetheless.

Surely, one could say that just a touch of the leader is not much of catch at all, that some form of tangible immobilization would be more indicative of catching the fish. I would agree to some extent. I would have rather held the fish by the bill, extracted the hook, and given it was our first marlin, probably even held it out of the water for a moment and snapped a few pictures while still being considerate of the fish's health. But on the other hand, in the realm of catch and release, recognizing a catch when the leader is merely touched is necessary and valuable and must be held valid. Because if catching the fish was the only goal, rather than catching and releasing the fish, it would have been just as easy, if not easier, for me to end the fight by burying a gaff into the side of beautiful fish rather than just touching the leader.

To me, the pictures did not matter too much, knowing the mental image will be with me forever. In particular, I can still call to mind one riveting image of the marlin flying parallel to the glassy ocean surface six feet below, graceful and timeless in the midst of chaos.

The three of us started our marlin hunting together, endured a heartbreaking encounter together, and if I had caught a marlin on my own it would not have been as sweet as doing it with Bill and Mike.

If a first time angler, or even relative novice, had caught the marlin, then I still would have been thrilled. Catching a marlin as a captain is in many ways more rewarding than being the angler. It was the first white marlin caught by a Nantucket charter boat in fourteen years, and that adds a nice feather to my professional cap and establishes some nice bragging rights, but it certainly would not have been the storybook ending we got.

This past summer Bill, Mike and I got another white, this time capping it off by billing the fish, removing the hook, and snapping a couple pictures of the four of us before releasing it alongside the boat. What endures about that fish is the way it appeared behind a teaser, its dorsal fin cutting a wake of its own while its bill slashed. The fish was angry and it swerved a wide *V* in the spread, with the clear intent to do some harm. It ate a circle-hook rigged ballyhoo and was off to the races, greyhounding a hundred yards in front of the boat as we hollered and chased in pursuit.

It has been a good couple years and our quest has been fulfilled. Bill has caught a couple marlin, and the three of us have established ourselves as Nantucket's most formidable marlin fishing team on and around the twenty fathom curve (though that distinction is somewhat dubious because we may be the only team in the league) and jealously has not tainted the events in the slightest. Though enough is enough, and when Bill, Mike and I go down to fish with John Brennan this winter, if we raise a blue marlin, I may "forget" that it is Bill's turn on the pitch bait.

5

Fishing Fathers

A Selfish Fishing Nut's Concerns on Adapting into a
Good Fishing Dad

When considering fishing and my family, I often wonder
what kind of fishing Dad I will be, and I am not altogether
confident I will be a good one. In realizing that I lack this noble
attitude toward others catching fish that some fishing guides
allegedly possesses (notice I am sticking with allegedly), I am
forced to confront the possibility that I lack the requisite attitude
of a superb fishing father. When I take Chick fishing, is it
possible that on some level I will be jealous of his fishing
success? Is it possible that I will resent the time it takes to tie his
knots and untangle the inevitable birds' nests when I could be
casting myself? Will I take him scup fishing and enjoy consistent
action or will I take him to my preferred flats and offer lectures
on patience and perseverance during the long waits in between
bites? When we are out fishing and he is too hot, too cold, too
tired or too hungry, will I do the right thing and point our boat
toward home, or will I badger him with fictionalized tales of the
toughness and fishing stamina I possessed in my youth, while
continuing to cast. Certainly, I like to think that my limitless love
for him and considerable patience will overcome any tendency

toward these less desirable behaviors, but I will need to closely monitor myself. My feelings toward Bill and his white marlin surely suggest that I have the capacity for magnanimity, and that is comforting.

While avoiding envy, I must embrace patience. I think most people who know me off the water would agree that I am a patient man, but I tend to fish with a degree of intensity that I do not exhibit much off the water. This intensity erodes portions of my patience. I can summon near limitless patience in waiting for a fish to bite, but patience for human error in the face of fish that may bite is another story, and though it often necessary that I summon some of this variety, it takes some effort to do so.

There is no better place to witness fathers and sons fishing than running a charter boat, especially in a place like Nantucket where the vast majority of customers are people on vacation who decide to do a little fishing, rather than people on a fishing trip. Over the past fifteen years I have seen every imaginable example of fishing father, the vast majority good, and some bad. Even the bad ones deserve some credit, after all, at least the sound decision to take their children fishing was made. But to truly do it right does take a little effort.

In my view the worst type of fishing dad, and thankfully the one I never have to worry about becoming, is the disinterested fishing dad. Not often, but more often than you would think, I get a dad who is clearly not interested in fishing, and not too interested in his kid's fishing. Most often, what they are concerned about is their business, and most often among disinterested dads, their business involves vague and intangible dealings involving vast amounts of other people's money, which is to say, not only are they sub-par parents, but they are responsible for the economic collapse of 2008, the Great Recession, Wall Street robbing Main Street and much of what is wrong in the United States today.

I am aware that most of these dads come from the financial sector because they spend the entire trip on their phone. In my early days it was a Motorola flip-phone, then a Blackberry, and now an iPhone. In some extreme cases even iPads or laptops are brought onboard. They spend the trip discussing interest rates, futures, short sales, margin calls, buyouts, Ponzi schemes, offshore accounts, and God knows what else, while their kid or kids catch fish. If two kids are involved, and they are small, occasionally Mike will need to press the father into service, asking him to help one child reel in a fish while he helps the other child (doubles being very common when trolling for bluefish), and they sullenly have to tear themselves away for a moment. In some circumstances, fewer these days than when cell phones first started popping up on the deck, we are out of range of cell service. Occasionally, this little wake-up call is all a father needs to start functioning as a decent dad, and upon their device being rendered useless they begin to take an interest in their kids and in the fishing. Unfortunately that is pretty rare, and the dads inquire as to when we will be back in cell phone range, the possibility of fishing closer to town, or how much longer the trip is going to last.

In no way do I mean to paint the entire financial industry as being unfit anglers or parents; many of my favorite and best customers have a career in finance. My friend and client Erik Passanante, is a fine angler and a superb fishing Dad. He spends innumerable hours on the water guiding his kids, his own angling aspirations always taking a back seat. Chris, his youngest son is in the second grade and currently fishes at the middle school level and his older son Ethan is in the sixth grade and fishes on par with many adults. Erik's job is centered on some financial instrument so complex and vague he never even deals with the people whose money is involved. He only deals with the bosses of the people who deal with the people whose money is involved. I am not sure how personally responsible he is for the economic meltdown and the ensuing recession, but he is such a good friend, good father and fine fishermen that I am willing to forgive him a few hundred billion dollars in government bailouts.

One day in the fall of 2012, I was running Erik's boat for him; we were fishing Great Point and enjoying the false albacore bonanza of that season. Onboard was Erik, his son Chris who must have been about six at the time, Erik's cousin, and Mike, who was invited along as a guest and was thoroughly enjoying fishing for fun while I worked. And I was working. I did consistent laps around the console, mostly boating, unhooking and releasing fish, and occasionally tying on a new Deadly Dick or making some other kind of tackle repair made necessary by the hard pulling albies. Erik and his cousin were hooked up more often than not, and Mike was doing serious business on the fly. Early in the trip, I had hooked a fish and let Chris reel it in, but the constant action was keeping me too busy to do it again. Not to be left out of the action, Chris helped himself to a rod and started casting. It is the rare angler that does not fall in love to some degree with his tackle, and Erik is no exception, though his priorities are clear when it comes to being a fishing Dad. He happily lets his sons give it a go with some very nice tackle that I would think twice about handing to Mike, and if he has second thoughts, he certainly doesn't show them. Chris was cut loose with a spinning rod, and shortly thereafter, started catching. Everybody was surprised and thrilled to look over and see Chris tight to a screaming albie, hooked all on his own. It was an impressive display. Chris had a big day on albies, just like everyone else, and battled a handful of them to the boat solo. Plenty of time on the water, some instruction, and perhaps more importantly, some freedom, are turning the Passanante boys into fine anglers.

Being able to offer competence, thorough knowledge, teaching and letting go, is a fine start for a fishing father, and probably a fine start for fathering in regard to many things. I have the knowledge, and I can teach it to Chick. Hopefully I can take a page from Erik's book and also know when to let go, and not to wince too much when Chick grabs my some of my cherished tackle, waves it around and declares he wants to fly fish.

While considering fishing and fathers, my thoughts consistently return to a trip with my own father. I was about thirteen and we were on a family vacation to the Florida Keys and my head was filled with dreams of all kinds of fish. I had read charter boat ads, guidebooks, and everything else fishing and Keys related that I could get me hands on, and needless to say, they offered a very optimistic view on what I could expect to catch fishing off the Florida Keys. I expected to catch several sailfish and probably a couple of marlin. I was blissfully unaware of the cost of guided fishing and I expressed a desire and expectation to do several days offshore, as well as a couple days on the flats. At some point, it was made clear to me that was not even a remote possibility, and we would do one offshore trip as a family.

It was late February, not a bad time to be sailfishing in the Keys, and during my evening strolls along the docks of Holiday Isle, Whale Harbor, and Bud and Mary's, there were plenty of boats flying sailfish flags, and a few sailfish on the dock, these being the last days before release mounts became the norm. One nice captain told me that if I had arrived last week, he would have guaranteed me a sailfish, but the bite had tapered off and he allowed a fifty-fifty shot: an early introduction to the "should have been here yesterday" sentiments that persist through a lifetime of fishing.

In any case, fifty-fifty wasn't bad, and I was looking forward to it. I remember virtually the whole charter boat fleet as impressive. Big Bertrams and Hatterases with tall tuna towers, outriggers, fighting chairs, and plenty of rods. They reminded me more of the private sportfishers on Nantucket's docks than the bluefish and striper charter boats. In my youth and narrow focus on the fishing accoutrements, I overlooked their age and their wear that would have quickly identified them as having a lot more in common with Nantucket's charter boats than gleaming new million dollar sportfishers across the marina, but in any case, their distinct offshore flavor excited me. I had a good feeling about many of the boats, and was leaning toward a trip with the captain who had offered the fifty-fifty shot on his large Hatteras.

While I was elsewhere, my father booked a trip. He only booked a half-day, a choice I was not pleased with, and it was on a boat I had previously overlooked. It was hidden at the end of the pier, and it was a real piece of shit. I have no idea how he settled on this boat, but I suspect that my father's love of a bargain may have been the determining factor. I may have registered my disappointment about both the choice of boats and the half versus full day, but pessimism before the trip even takes place is not my style and I still looked forward to the trip.

When we arrived in the morning, there was some kind of mechanical trouble. I recall a few parts of the engine being spread around the deck and the dock, and the motor not starting. The captain and the mate were working on it, and my father and brother joined the effort. My brother, Tim, was barely in middle school but he has been something of a mechanical genius from a very early age. I don't think the captain and mate would have gotten us off the dock, but with help from my Dad and brother we were off in an uncomfortable amount of diesel smoke only about an hour late.

We started to troll and two subsurface lines were put out off the stern on some kind of downrigger or weight and two surface lines were put out on the sides. We were told the subsurface lines got more bites, and my brother and I each chose one, and my father would get the two surface lines.

After a short time trolling, one of the surface lines got bit. During the choosing up of lines, it was very clear that the surface lines were my father's. I instantly regretted choosing my rod instead of the surface lines, and fully expected my father to reel in the fish. I was shocked and delighted when he hustled me out of my chair to take the fish despite the fact it was on his line. In my youthful exuberance, I did not hesitate to rob him of his fish, and I went to work. The mate excited me tremendously when he said it might be a sailfish, but shortly afterward it jumped revealing itself to be a large barracuda. This was only slightly disappointing at the time, and I was happy to fight the large barracuda. I brought it in, and for some reason, they killed it. This didn't upset me at all, my catch and release ethics not having been fully formed and being of an age when killing something and bringing it home was very appealing.

We ended up catching a couple more kingfish, and then casting some lures on old and faulty tackle to some smaller barracuda close to what I believe was Alligator Reef Light. I was old enough to realize that you didn't always catch what you wanted, I was old enough to understand I should probably be grateful for the trip and the chance, but I was too young to act how I knew I should. I tried to take some comfort in my barracuda. It was the largest fish I had ever caught to that point, and it was a new species to me, which always excites, but it was not a sailfish, and then, as now, I was of the opinion that billfish have no equal. I tried to smile through some photos and put on a good face about the whole experience, though my mother sensed something was wrong. Her questions elicited my disappointment in the lack of a sailfish, and I am little embarrassed to say even twenty years later, some tears. She was peeved and reminded me that I was lucky just because I got to go fishing, which I truly needed no reminding about, having been already reminding myself of that for the entire boat ride home and the photo session that followed.

Seeing the boats coming home from full days later that afternoon, many flying sailfish flags, didn't help. For years I was mad at my father about the trip, and it did not abate when I gained some experience in Florida sailfishing. I was angry he picked the worst looking boat on the dock shoved in the corner. I was of the opinion he should have picked a boat that had returned from a successful day of sailfishing, their competence having been proven, and instead we were on a boat that looked as if it hadn't moved in a decade. I was upset that we fished for a half day, when I thought a full day would have brought us out further, where we would have probably encountered the frenzied feeding of any number of billfish. As the years passed and I learned more about Florida sailfishing, I realized that prime sailfish habitat was easily accessible in a half-day. However, this knowledge did little to mitigate my feelings, as I then wondered why the hell we were trolling dead baits instead of flying kites, why our trip was spent clearly well inshore of the reef line and drop-off where sails were likely to be found, why we were trolling subsurface lines at all, and another thing that only occurs to me now, why I caught that barracuda without getting cut off. I suspect we were trolling with wire leaders, certainly not ideal for sailfish.

My ex post facto knowledge of Florida sailfishing made me mad at the captain for clearly not targeting sailfish in any reasonable manner. I am not sure if this was a blatant misrepresentation on his part, telling my father we were going sailfishing and then taking us on a wild goose chase, trolling some dead baits around inside the reef, or if my father's bargaining included some advice to the captain like, just bend the rods a couple times and everybody will be happy. So I was mad at my father also for either failure to do his homework and get a trustworthy and experienced sailfish captain or his complicit acceptance of a half-assed trip. My anger was assuaged to some degree by time and maturity and almost erased years later when I actually caught a sailfish, eventual success being the only good way to overcome past fishing failures, though I still haven't completely let it go. I would forgive my father for mistakenly thinking I was less of a fishing snob in middle school and assuming I would be happy with a fish, and not just a billfish, but if I found out that clown of a captain had represented the trip he took us on as a serious sailfish expedition I would be tempted to give him a good beating next time I pass through Islamorada. Taking advantage of the fishing dreams of youngsters is a high crime with no statute of limitations.

But now, in thinking about the whole affair in terms of fathers fishing with their sons, my thoughts are not about mistakes that may have been made in the planning stages. I think about my father, not hesitating for a moment, insisting that I take the rod with the buzzing drag. Mistakes in the planning can always be second-guessed. There are only degrees and percentages, and no boat offered a guaranteed billfish, and there was no right or wrong, only shades of grey. The only black and white decision of the entire thing was that my father let me reel in that fish, even though it had bit his rod.

It will come as no surprise that seeing a father give his son a fish is fairly commonplace now. But that fishing trip in Islamorada happened long before I became a charter captain, long before I knew the protocol of fathers and sons on charter trips. The generosity of the gesture impressed me then and it impresses me now.

The whole episode is an apt microcosm of fishing with my father. At times, especially as I got a little older and developed even further into an uncompromising fishing nut, his decisions would aggravate me, his cavalier attitude toward tackle and rigging would infuriate me, and his lack of desire to spend huge amounts of time and money chasing large fish all over the larger ocean disappointed me. And now that I am little older still, and considering what makes a good fishing father, I find myself aspiring to be near as good as he was. He was generous with his time, during which he seldom handled a rod himself once my brother and I were old enough to do it on our own. He was extremely patient, quick to smile and laugh, and found greater joy just in fishing with his sons than in anything we happened to catch or not catch.

Mostly, these are the dads you see on the water. A fishing dad and family out for a good time, catching a few fish, having a few laughs. It is not difficult to be at your best while you are fishing on vacation, and being around this kind of happiness often is one of the lesser-known joys of being a charter captain.

Occasionally though, instead of generous dads handing rods to sons, I will get a father who wants to catch his children's fish. This is usually the case with fish-crazed dads, who, to be honest, I sometimes see more of myself in than the magnanimous fathers who are happy to take the role of a fan in virtually all of the action. Often these dads jump into action on their observation, real or imagined, that their children are doing a poor job and without their assistance (or complete assumption of the fight), the fish will be lost. They decide their son is not reeling fast enough, or that he is reeling too fast, or that the line is twisting against the drag, or it is rubbing against the boat, and they quickly relieve their son of the rod, usually in order to "demonstrate" proper technique. I am a prime candidate for pulling a stunt like this. Being both very excited by the thought of catching fish and intolerant of poor angling technique puts me at high risk to relieve a child of their rod mid-fight. While I don't consider this to be as much of an angling and parenting sin as the disinterested Dad (after all the kid wasn't fighting the fish right!), I certainly do not aspire to it.

I take some comfort in thinking that I may have learned my lesson during an episode with my wife that I am still ashamed of. It happened when Liz came down to Pine Island to visit and fish with me in the middle of my month long fishing sabbatical a few years ago. I had been having excellent results tossing soft plastics on jig heads among a certain couple of stretches of mangroves, resulting in a nice mixed bag of snook and redfish. To have much success with this technique, one needs to be a pretty accurate caster. Most bites come very tight to the mangroves, and every cast is little game of chicken, testing how close you are willing to aim, and how much nerve you have to let your lure continue to fly toward the roots waiting to ensnare it. I determined Liz was not ready for this, and I stand by this as just good sense rather than fishing snobbery. An inexperienced caster is going to have a long, frustrating and expensive day throwing lures at mangroves. We went to a little stretch where I had been particularly lucky, but instead of plastics on jig heads, we had some live shrimp, and instead of repeated casts, she could make one good one and then wait.

She threw her shrimp and bobber into a nice fishy-looking place along the mangroves, and mere moments later, the bobber disappeared without hesitation. She hooked the fish, and it made a run past the boat away from the mangroves. It was a nice redfish, the snook being more likely to try and regain safety in the mangroves and jump. She really did a nice job for the first part of the fight. She halted the fish's run, and kept tension as she retrieved it. She had it nearly to the net, but in a classic redfish maneuver, it starting diving powerfully for the bottom in a rapid set of direction changes around the stern. It was not the easiest situation in which to keep a tight line, lead the fish in a sensible way, and keep the rod and line clear of the motor and the boat. My wife was struggling with it, and, it being one of her first fish, she was a little panicked, and in my fish-on state of excitement bordering on hysteria, I determined that she was not up to the task. I relieved her of the rod. In my defense I think she was relieved more than angry, and I danced around the stern and the motor with the fish for a few moments, eventually working it to a more manageable position, at which time I returned the rod to my wife while I netted, photographed and released her nice redfish. It was a nice fish, a nice catch, a nice moment, and I don't think my wife was the least bit angered or upset that I assisted her for a minute, but I immediately regretted relieving her of the rod at a critical moment. It has left a sour enough taste in my mouth that I believe I have learned my lesson and I will let my son fight his own fights.

Of course, it is also possible to take it too far in the other direction, and perhaps I am being too hard on myself. My wife was truly pleased to catch that redfish. She was a beginner and had no knowledge that by touching the rod I eliminated the red as an official catch in the eyes of the International Game Fish Association and any tournament, and if she had known she still would not have cared. Whereas, losing the fish would have been lame. The photos or knowledge of a caught fish are more important than what the IGFA says at least ninety-nine percent of the time. Perhaps if I had not relieved her of the rod, the leader would have severed on the propeller and she would have returned to New England with a sad story of one that got away rather than a very nice caught redfish, with which she only needed a moment's help when the fish went under the boat near the engine.

I will try to avoid taking the rod from my children's hands when not asked, but what to do when the child does ask to be relieved is another question. This, I believe, is the only question to this point that presents a real philosophical dilemma. The obvious answer, is of course, take the rod from a child when they ask you to take it, but prematurely relieving your child of rod, even when they ask to be relieved, may not be best. I have seen fathers stand over sons (or daughters) begging to be relieved of rods or let out of fighting chairs, claiming the fish is too big or too strong (or in the case of wire line, the tackle itself being quite a fight), and fathers reluctant or refusing to take over.

Most times this pays off. The son continues despite some complaining, lands the fish by himself, and perhaps even learns a life lesson on perseverance or a belief in oneself. The children that go through this once are usually eager to catch another fish, and seldom afterward do they want or require adult assistance. It can be a touchy situation though and at times it results in a crying child mad at his or her dad for the duration of the trip, or perhaps in the extreme, a child who no longer wants to fish with his or her dad. It is difficult situation to be sure. The answer lies in the middle ground, first in not being too quick to pull the plug, while in the other hand knowing your child enough to step in prior to any real damage.

A ray of hope that one can be a fishing nut and also as a good fishing father comes from my mother. I am not sure you would call her a total fishing nut; she prioritizes a number of things over fishing, but she certainly has the capacity for it. Her father and my grandfather, Captain Bob Ruley, was a fishing nut. He ran a Rybovich out of Nantucket in the dawn of offshore sportfishing. From the same waters where I am now lucky to find an occasional white marlin, he regularly returned with behemoth broadbill swordfish. The boat wintered in Florida and the Bahamas, and he would spend those months chasing marlin and sailfish. In his later years he didn't miss a fishing opportunity. He often patrolled Nantucket's beaches for blues and bass, and even teamed up with my mother to fish in local pond tournaments put on by the Nantucket Anglers' Club.

My grandfather and my mother as well as a couple dozen more local fishing nuts, would hit the ponds all weekend to see who could amass the most points as determined by different points per ounce, per species: pickerel were one point per ounce, white perch two, yellow perch three, and pumpkinseed sunfish four. It was on these ponds that my mother introduced me to fishing. Long before I started boating with my dad, she toted me around in search of perch and pickerel, taught me how to tie on the hook, how to bait it, how long to wait after your bobber went down. Before long, I got to accompany my mother when she fished the tournaments, competing for myself in the junior division. It was during those Anglers' Club tournaments that I got my first taste of the extent to which people would go to catch a fish. Fishing with my father was mostly pleasant boat rides on warm, sunny, summer days. Fishing with my mother meant if there was a rumored white perch bite and sunrise at the Massasoit Bridge in Madaket, you could bet we would have our bobbers in the water there fifteen minutes before the sun came up. If it was raining you did not roll over and go back to bed, you put on a jacket. We were chasing perch with a couple dollars on the line, but we may as well have been fishing the Bisbees Black & Blue, and it certainly was no less fun.

While my father was the epitome of an easy going fishing dad, anything mercurial in my fishing, and my character, comes from my mother. Sometimes we do not admit it, but we are very much alike in a number of ways. At times these shared traits and interests make us get along like two peas in a pod, and other times, we get along like Ali and Frazier, content to overlook what we see of ourselves in the other, and batter each other mercilessly.

She still chases pond fish, along with a group of fishing nut ladies whose big annual event is the Anglers' Club's ladies-only Happy Hookers pond tournament. The all have red sweatshirts that say "Happy Hookers," on the front, and they seem to get a laugh out of wearing them around town. For me, fishing with my mother today is as much fun as it ever was. Sometimes I will call her and see if she wants to spend a few hours on the water. She usually jumps at the chance, eager again to be a fishing parent. She is happy to weigh in with opinions on how I should spend my time, and she has made no secret of her low opinion of sportfishing as a career choice, but when she has a bonito on the line, and the reel is screaming, she is proud to have a fishing nut for a son. It is clear to both of us, at least for a little while, that we are hard on each other only because we see each other's potential and have high expectations. I am happy in realizing that my mother is a nut, just like me, and our bond is a powerful one.

Between my easy-going father and my hard charging mother, I had two fantastic, though divergent fishing parents. From years on the water I have seen many more examples of excellent fishing parents and an unfortunate handful of poor ones. Finally, my favorite fishing scene in all of literature explores the father-son dynamic in the extreme. While *The Old Man and Sea* is widely regarded as the best fishing book in existence, and by many as the best book, it is a scene from Hemingway's lesser-known and much less acclaimed *Islands in the Stream* that is my favorite.

Young David battles a grander broadbill off Bimini while his father, Tomas Hudson, drives the boat. It magnificently details their departure from Bimini in the morning, to the strike and the drop-back thick with dread, apprehension and exquisite anticipation, through the five-hour plus battle, to the return home. There is beautiful imagery of the Gulfstream and wonderful dialogue. It is the best portrayal in existence of the fear, the tension, and the teamwork that shape the atmosphere of a big game cockpit with a fish on the line. Most importantly, it offers exquisite and realistic details of the struggle between a boy and a fish. David's brother, young Tom, questions his father repeatedly as the fight lingers if letting David continue to fight the fish is a good idea. Through the hours, David suffers through chaffed and bleeding feet, blisters and chafing from the harness, and general fatigue, but he is allowed to go on. Hudson quite aptly points out that they do not only have to worry about the physical damage the fish will do to David, but also the more lasting mental damage perhaps caused by taking the fish away from him. Hudson offers the following, "You're an awfully good boy, Tommy. But please know that I would have stopped this long ago except that I know that if David catches this fish he'll have something inside him for all his life and it will make everything else easier."

After six hours of fighting the fish, the hook pulls with the fish barely beyond the reach of the gaff. It was the days before catch and release, and there are certainly plenty of pictures out there of Papa standing next to a dead fish on the dock. And I may be reading too much into it, or merely trying to put a positive spin on a heartbreaking event, but I like to think Hemingway is illustrating a large fish alive and swimming away after the battle is more wonderful, more telling, and more fitting than a dead and colorless one hanging at the dock. This view is bolstered by David's concern for the fish's welfare after they part ways.

The lesson fishing fathers should take from this, is that by their early teens children should be pitted against a monstrous gamefish, preferably over a thousand pounds, and be pushed to the absolute brink of human endurance while sustaining significant physical injury. Or perhaps not. A six-hour battle with a swordfish over a thousand pounds is not a fight any of us are likely to see their son make. Nevertheless, I enjoy Hudson's line thoroughly, and perhaps fishing with your children is about giving them something to take with them. Perhaps it will not be some kind of interior toughness that comes from enduring an epic fish fight, maybe it will be an appreciation for the natural world, an introduction to a wholesome and lifelong pursuit, or maybe just pleasant memories. For the human experience is often difficult and sometimes painful, and maybe, by taking them fishing, they will have something inside them for all their life and it will make everything else easier.

6

Scallop Crazy

I suppose at some point every Nantucket writer must weigh in on scalloping, especially one who writes about the outdoors and who has spent many of the last several winters out scalloping.

Scalloping is currently the most nostalgic and romantic of Nantucket professions, a throwback, where men and women take to the harbor in small boats to simply and honestly ply a living from the sea. From their efforts, diners enjoy some of the world's most delectable seafood. Numerous articles, as well as the book *Scallop Season* by Jim Patrick with photos by Rob Benchley, celebrate the profession. *Scallop Season* sits proudly on most island bookshelves including my parents. I haven't actually read it, and to be perfectly honest I don't have any plans to read it, but I will not rule it out. Perhaps some day I will look back on my scalloping career as romantic and reading it will provide a nice stroll down memory lane. But for the time being, I get my fill of scalloping without reading about it.

While Nantucketers have had a long love affair with scallops and scalloping, much of the romance of it is lost on me (and I suspect on many of those who actually do it). Going out day after winter day in all types of conditions to drag around heavy, weighted nets called dredges, then haul them back in, dump them out and sort through seaweed, mud, muck, rocks and one-year old scallops, hoping to find the two-year old scallops with which to fill your five boxes, and then repeating the process as many times as necessary is hard and not terribly exciting work. I actively look forward to giving it up. When I was struggling in college or law school, the thought of never having to go scalloping again was powerful motivation. I have been very thankful in recent years when Nantucket High has needed the temporary services of an English or history teacher and I was able to leave the cold boat for the warm classroom. But, despite all this, I now find myself back at it.

Today, for the first time in my scalloping career, I contemplated the possibility that I may continue scalloping for years to come. Perhaps start doing it by choice, rather than as a last resort in order to make a few dollars in the winter. A conscious choice made at least in some part out of desire rather than necessity, regarding it as more than a fill-in money-maker for the off-season. This morning was absolutely gorgeous, the harbor was glassy calm, and the colors in sky as the sun came up over Monomy and Shimmo were spectacular. It was cold, with the temperature in the low thirties, but that does not matter much at all when there is no wind and your face isn't pelted with freezing, stinging salt spray as you cruise. Whatever chill you may feel will evaporate quickly once you start working. With no wind to steal your body heat and the hard work, you may as well be working in a temperature-controlled office. Needless to say, the scenery is much better.

Additionally, the scalloping was pretty good today. To this point, scalloping in 2012 has been something of a disappointment. Predictions about a good year were very common throughout the spring and summer, but for whatever reason, things started to look a little leaner in the fall. Reports on family scalloping in October (before the commercial season starts November 1st) were not great, and by the time opening day for commercial season rolled around nobody was too optimistic. My Dad and I started in one spot this morning, and we were driving to another. We had already been to both spots this season, and both had some scallops but not too many. On the way I suggested we try a dredge in my "secret spot." He knew where I was talking about because there is only one scalloping spot that can be called "mine", and though calling it a secret is a bit of a stretch, it is not among the most popular scalloping spots in the harbor and that makes it secret enough.

It is extremely rare that I offer unsolicited advice when scalloping with my dad. For me to advise my father on scalloping is similar to me offering some football strategy to Bill Belichick or giving Lefty Kreh some pointers on fly casting. My dad is not a limitless trove of outdoor know-how. When I developed an interest and desire to start hunting, I had to look elsewhere for tutelage. His entire hunting experience amounted to one afternoon adventure in high school. He and two friends rode around in a truck with a shotgun, and upon seeing a pheasant, his friend shot at it without leaving his seat. My father found the ringing in his ears painful and the whole experience unsavory and never hunted again. My father spent countless hours on the water with my brother and me, introducing us to saltwater fishing, but the real draw to him was time on the boat and time with his family; fishing was just the vehicle. When fishing became my passion, it wasn't too long before my knowledge and know-how equaled, and then surpassed, his. There were times growing up when I held this against him. How was I supposed to learn to hunt if he didn't take me and why were we always going bluefishing when the tuna, sharks and marlin of my dreams were just offshore? Of course, this was a totally unjustified attitude given the countless hours of fatherly instruction I received on many things unrelated to hunting and big game fishing, but children tend to expect a lot of their parents, as I suppose parents expect a lot of their children.

When it comes to scalloping, though, there is no question that my father is elite. He knows all the spots and all the finer points of scalloping methodology. He can cull quicker than most men while still steering the boat exactly where he wants. He adjusts the speed of the boat and the weights on the dredges to fish perfectly, catching as many scallops and as little of everything else as possible. If there are scallops to be found, he finds them, and he catches them quickly. One of the joys of scalloping with my father is that we are always home early, returning to the dock to enjoy the rest of the day sometimes hours ahead of other scallopers. My father has about fifty years of scalloping experience along with a passion for shellfishing that may rival my passion for sportfishing. Under these circumstances it is easy to understand why I seldom offer advice and why there is only one spot called "mine." He had already scalloped in every spot before I was even born.

The spot became known as my secret spot because four or five years ago, I was scalloping on my own. My father had gone to Florida for some nice weather and golf, and I went to the spot on my own accord. I received no advice from my father, or my younger brother who is just as scallop-crazy as my father, and got my limit of five boxes every day for two weeks. I think they were both surprised I got *any* scallops on my own, let alone several limits from an unlikely spot, and honestly, I surprised myself. I went there entirely because it was out of the wind and it is a good striper spot. I figured that if stripers liked it there it was a healthy, attractive little piece of water and scallops might like it there too. It worked, but I have since applied that logic in scouting out several more spots with almost no success whatsoever so I think that first time was coincidental.

Despite disappointing yields in every season since, I still have fond feelings and a predilection for the spot. And this

74

morning, as we motored from a spot we had just determined was mediocre to another spot we already knew to be mediocre, as we were passing close by my spot, I uncharacteristically offered some advice and suggested we throw a test dredge there. Having nothing to lose, my dad agreed, made a slight detour, and threw a dredge. It came up with a nice layer of scallops in the bottom, and we decided to throw all eight dredges and make a full tow. The dredges came up with almost two full boxes of the biggest, most beautiful scallops we had seen all season. We spent the morning pulling an unexpected amount of surprisingly large scallops from a spot we had to ourselves. I felt good about it, but my dad, with his passion for shellfish, was over the moon. His excitement was on par with what I would have experienced if he had accurately told me where to find dozens of hungry white marlin. He could not contain himself and celebrated our good fortune as we worked.

As he scooped handfuls of big adult scallops off the culling board he cackled, "Look at this! 'Lets throw a dredge in my secret spot,' you said, Oh boy, look at this! We are going to get our limit. If you had told me were going to come in with ten boxes at ten o'clock in December a month ago, I would have told you you were crazy!" He laughed, and I smiled and laughed too, finding his enthusiasm for scallops infectious for perhaps the first time. I enjoyed, for once, being responsible for a little bit of our scalloping success rather than just relying on my father.

There, surrounded by harbor beaches still streaked with little snow drifts and the colors of the sunrise having given way to a bright and cloudless blue winter sky I was struck by the unruffled beauty of my current workplace. A beauty intensified by the knowledge that it is not being divided among countless visitors and tourists, it is there only for the handful of scallopers, the real Nantucketers. Faced with this beauty and the intense satisfaction that comes with a day of hard and productive physical labor, not to mention a few hundred dollars worth of scallops in our boxes, I considered always going. I wondered how many places I would rather be than on Nantucket Harbor, and none were quick to come to mind.

Since I have been working on a strong dislike of scalloping for about a decade and a half, these sentiments were certainly odd. Upon further reflection, I realized that from November through March there are millions of places I would rather be, namely any productive warm-water flat or piece of ocean in the entire world. I also realized that any fond feelings I was developing would evaporate very quickly the next day I scalloped with a northeast wind and perhaps some freezing rain to accompany it, at which point you could add almost anywhere indoors (including a dentist's chair but excluding prison) to the places I would rather be.

My preference for warm weather, fin-fish over shellfish, and a classroom to a scallop boat makes me an outcast in the family. My father and brother are scallop crazy to the point that if scallops inexplicably become worthless, I suspect the two of them will continue to do it just for fun. It was a tradition for my brother, even in early elementary school, to be able to skip school on the first day of November, or at least arrive late, in order to join my father on that first day of commercial season. I do not recall if the invitation was extended to me or not. I think it was at least the first few years, but even then I preferred a warm classroom to Nantucket Harbor in November.

I would occasionally be cajoled into going on holidays and school vacations through high school, taking a strong dislike to it almost immediately, but my first introduction to any serious scalloping was during college, and it serves as pretty good example of why communism does not work.

My Christmas break lasted from mid-December through virtually the entire month of January, and I was consistently enlisted in those years to accompany my father scalloping. I was not paid anything. I spent the whole summer running the family charter boat, the *Topspin*, and the winter break scalloping. I never saw any paychecks, but I never saw tuition bills either, a deal which quite obviously worked out in my favor so I had little standing to complain. However, I knew those tuition bills were going to be taken care of regardless of how successful we were at scalloping, and in my mind I would actively root for either such poor scalloping that my father would give it up by December or January when I got home, vicious cold streaks below twenty-eight degrees so it would not be legal to go, or just about anything else that would keep me off the water. In my better moments, I realized this to be the mindset of a spoiled, lazy, little shit, but that realization did not vanquish the thoughts from mind completely.

Once we got out on the water, I knew the quickest way to be done with the whole thing was to get our limit and be back in, so even with my poor attitude I was usually a decent hand if not pleasant company. My mood was no mystery to my father, and at times, when the sun was out and it really wasn't a bad day on the water, he would ask me about my views on scalloping. Like a bacon aficionado questioning a vegetarian, he really could not understand how anybody, let alone his own son, could dislike scalloping.

"Matt, do you like scalloping?"

"No Dad, I can't stand it."

"But what about a day like today, when the sun is out, it gets a little warm, isn't it nice to be out here on a day like today?"

"Not really."

"What else would you be doing?"

"Reading, cooking, duck hunting, living in Florida, anything."

"Come on, its not so bad."

"Yes it is. It is terrible."

On the frequent days when the weather was bad, the questions were never about the inherent joys of scalloping. Then the questions were about my temperature. He would ask, "Matt, are you cold?"

I would unfailingly and truthfully, answer yes.

"What is cold?" he would say.

I would reply, "My feet, hands, nose, face and ears."

"Come on," he would say, "your face is cold, how is your face cold?"

I would wonder how anybody's face wouldn't be cold, given that saltwater slightly above freezing was intermittently splashing into it most of the morning. I am not sure why he always asked if I was cold, perhaps to make sure I was not in danger of hypothermia or frostbite, but I consistently answered that I was cold, very cold, and we never went in so that explanation doesn't hold water. I think we were both cold, and there was not much either of us could do about it. Eventually, we began to both get a laugh out of it.

My dad would say, "Are you cold?"

I would say, "Yes," and the more parts of me that were cold, the funnier it was.

"What is cold?"

"My toes, feet, ankles, shins, calves, knees, thighs, stomach, back, shoulders, arms, elbows, hands, fingers, neck, chin, lips, nose, cheeks, ears, forehead and eyeballs."

He would exclaim with a smile, "Your eyes are cold? I never heard of anybody's eyeballs being cold!"

"Well, my eyes are cold. Every time I open them, the cold wind stings them," and he would lose it. Cold eyeballs really got him going. Cold eyeballs were always good for a laugh.

Looking back, it was probably one of those times, standing behind the culling board with my father, both of us freezing our asses off in a small boat in crappy weather, laughing like idiots about my cold eyeballs, rather than on a sunny day, that I first considered that scalloping maybe was not all bad.

Of course, I was not quick to admit that, and when the weather improved and we were back to scalloping under the sun and my father would ask me if I still disliked scalloping, I would still unhesitatingly reply yes, but my position was starting to waiver, and I think my Dad knew that even before I did.

Eventually, I was out of school, equipped with a fancy set of degrees that could keep me out of scallop boats forever. Yet after a few unfulfilling stints in the practice of law and a couple even less appealing jobs, I spent most of the winters of my late twenties scalloping, and after taking the last two years off, one to teach English and one to stay home with my young son, I am back. No longer a kid helping his Dad when he is home from school, but a real scalloper.

Making a good day's pay out on the water rather than stuck in an office with a warm November sun shining down on you certainly isn't bad, and a few laughs with Dad is great, but it certainly wasn't enough (and isn't for that matter) to make it my first choice of winter activities. A few different factors came together keeping me on the water those first few years. First, my plan in those days was to find a winter job sportfishing, either as the captain or mate of a private boat or running a charter boat someplace south. Scalloping was a nice fallback option, and when the phone rang, which it seldom did, I could drop everything, hop on a plane, and be fishing in no time. Scalloping is a nice flexible job. The next factor was the day's pay. With tuition out of the way, I couldn't really be expected to scallop out of a sense of family responsibility anymore. Actually, that is not true. I am still expected to scallop largely out of family responsibility, but now I get paid too. While the pay can fluctuate anywhere from terrible to very good, it is toward the favorable end of the spectrum often enough to keep me going.

Finally, the hours are fantastic. When I was a kid, my grandparents had a shanty in the back of their garage and my father and grandfather opened their own scallops. After they got in, got warm, and had some lunch, they went back to work: standing for hours in the shanty, cutting then separating the muscle from the two shells, cleaning the guts off it, and tossing the clean little scallop into a bowl and the shells and guts into a trash bin. But ever since I have been involved, the opening gets done for us. We take our boxes of unopened scallops straight from the boat to Evie Sylvia's, drop them off, and return hours later for a bucket of only the edible muscles (often called eyes, though the scallop has many other beautiful little blue eyes lining the interior of the shell that get discarded as "guts") and empty boxes.

Not opening your own makes you sort of a dilettante among scallopers, but that is a small price to pay. The profession is brutal enough that anybody who has a clue doesn't question your work ethic at all once they learn you are a scalloper regardless of whether you open your own or not. Not being quite as resolute as the guys who catch and open their own is a pretty small price to pay to be done with work hours earlier. In the early part of the season sometimes I am done by nine am, getting home by mid-morning is usually no problem, and anything after noon is pretty rare. Having a tremendous amount of the day free suits me.

In my first years as a scalloper, I would often get home and warm up only to head back outdoors, spending entire afternoons walking through marshes, trying to jump shoot a few ducks, or perhaps sitting over decoys. I would willingly and happily venture out into cold and bad weather, walking miles or, even worse, sitting still shivering, in pursuit of ducks, an endeavor that, at best, would yield one delectable dinner, but only after considerably more work (I couldn't drop dead ducks anywhere to be cleaned and made ready for cooking). I was reluctant to brave the same weather for a good paycheck and as many delectable dinners as I could stand. It is interesting where our hearts and priorities are.

If I was not hunting, there was plenty of time for woodworking or other various home improvement projects. The first winter I was dating Liz, I would scallop and then often come home and prepare meals. When you have most of the day at your disposal, dinner can be quite luxurious, and I spent a big chunk of that winter cooking my way into my wife's heart.

There is also writing. During one of my first winters as a scalloper, I completed the manuscript of a novel that I had been dabbling with for years. It turns out that it isn't much of novel, at least in its current state, and it now sits unpublished in my file cabinet and on my hard drive and it will remain that way perhaps forever or at least until I undertake some serious rewriting. But just finishing it was something, and knowing that I could in fact write a book, or least a collection of sentences as long as a book, validated more writing.

Of course, that validation applied only to me. Even after the moderate success of *Fishing Nantucket*, my wife and parents do not regard me as a real writer, and I'm not sure they regard writing as a real profession. In my twenties when I said I would be spending the afternoon writing, the look on my mother's face suggested that was akin to spending the afternoon eating potato chips and playing Nintendo.

For one week of my first full scallop season, I was feeling uninspired as far as writing went, or perhaps I was just being lazy. I decided the answer was to reread the greatest novel ever written, *Lonesome Dove*, hoping that some of Larry McMurtry's genius would rub off on me. After all, one thing all great writers have in common is that they are voracious readers. Every day after I came home from scalloping, I would build a fire in the fireplace, align myself in front of it in a recliner, and dive into *Lonesome Dove*.

Upon seeing this for a couple of days, my mother became apoplectic. I am not sure if my mother is against leisure time in general, but I am sure she is against me having any. Even during the height of summer, when I am fishing about twelve hours a day, seven days a week, leaving little time for anything but going home, grabbing a bite and crawling into bed to pass out before getting up to do it again, she has suggested several times in the past, with a straight face, that I consider a night job. Seeing me comfortable and reading mid-day was almost too much for her to take. I foolishly enraged her further by claiming that I was "working", because all writers needed to read, and I was a writer. A couple showdowns on the topic of mid-day reading were all the inspiration I needed to begin packing my bag for the library each day after scalloping to go get some writing done. Staying at home to read or write would only have been done with great disregard for my personal safety.

This season, I balance scalloping and taking care of my son. The little guy goes to daycare two days a week, giving me just a taste of the old days and though Liz seems to share my mother's views on daytime reading, duck season is coming up and I will get some time in marshes. On the other days I retrieve my son from my Mom or Aunt and spend the rest of day chasing him around. Given the rigors of chasing around a mobile one and a half-year old, for the first time in my scalloping career, I may be inclined to say, "Dad, maybe we should make one more tow."

How much scalloping is in my future is hard to say. Despite the success and pleasant feelings, I am still not ready to commit. I would much prefer to spend the winter teaching in a classroom, writing at a desk, wading a bonefish flat, or trolling the tranquil Pacific off Costa Rica. But if scalloping is in my future, I will be thankful for Nantucket's natural beauty, the satisfaction derived from hard work, and the time I get to spend with my dad, and I will not complain. At least not until my eyeballs get cold.

7

The Separation of Fish and Plate

Advice on Dinner, Fishing, and Fishing for Dinner

I am going fishing tomorrow, and if I catch a bluefish under five pounds, I am going to bring it home and cook it for my son. I have actually been thinking about it for a while, and I hope to put him on a fairly heavy diet of bluefish. When we first introduced the little guy to food, he seemed to love everything we gave him. He devoured peas, carrots, spinach, and variety of other healthy foods with gusto. He got a little older and I made him food-processed dinners of chicken or pot roast with lots of vegetables. He loved them. Now that we are onto solid food, the little guy has become a little bit picky. I have no basis for comparison since he is my first child, and really the first baby I have paid any serious attention to, and I think in the overall scheme of things he is probably still a decent eater. Even so getting eggs, chicken or beef into him is difficult.

He is growing so fast that I feel a constant pressure to keep up with his caloric needs, and I have a slight fear that if he somehow ends up a few calories short it is going to rob him of precious inches or musculature. I imagine him to be a parking meter, but instead of quarters, I need to continually fill him with protein or a meter maid will come along and ticket his size. Given my own physique, probably the last thing I need to worry about is bulking up the little guy, and I should try to keep him slender and encourage a fruit and vegetable heavy diet, but like most fathers I know, I fully expect Chick to be an NFL quarterback, and he is going to need tremendous size and strength. To that end, I need the little guy to have plenty of protein, and bluefish may be the healthy answer.

My mother has a dog, named Captain, and he has become an icon down on Straight Wharf in the summer. When he was a puppy, he used to occasionally meet me at the dock, and I used to slice him off some bluefish cheeks to eat. My mother objected briefly, because she objects to everything I do on principle. However, she quickly realized that giving her puppy fresh, high protein, low fat, organic, wild food, that happened to be free was a far better alternative to bagged or canned dog food. He took an immediate liking to it, as I imagine I would too if my culinary experience to that point was limited to dry little pellets smelling of liver. He graduated from cheeks to filets, and eventually started moving from our filet stand down the dock begging bluefish scraps from all the charter boats on Straight Wharf. I would say that it is not uncommon for him to consume two or three bluefish a day in the summer and he is well known around the dock as the bluefish-eating dog.

As far as dogs go, he is pretty striking. He is a pure lab, but he is so tall people often surmise that he is lab mixed with a larger breed, and he is lean. His coat is shiny and lustrous. I do not know how dog years work, but I think he may be past the century mark. He is pretty slow these days, but when he was younger he could really move. Watching him run was more like watching a horse than another dog. I attribute at least some these qualities to bluefish, and while I do not think it wise to base Chick's entire diet on a black lab's, I am confident that bluefish is good.

Bluefish are a fast-growing fish in the middle of the food chain, and that is generally not a recipe for mercury build-up. I am not one that pays close attention to what levels of what particular substance are in what. Paying attention to that sort of thing will drive you mental, and pretty soon you will not be allowed to eat anything. However, since I plan on feeding it to my one-year old, a little research will make me (and his mother) rest easier. A quick internet search revealed the only thing to potentially worry about in bluefish is PCBs. After another internet search, I found that PCBs are too complicated to understand from a simple internet search. The whole business is very vague and barely mentioned and if I searched any kind of food I would find some kind of warning about something, so I will chalk this up as not concerning at all.

I am going to feed him a small bluefish because I regard feeding anybody a large bluefish as cruel. The fact that small ones are of higher food quality than larger ones is not uncommon in fish. I haven't personally eaten a lot of large sharks, but I am told that once makos or threshers get past the two-hundred-pound mark, their quality as table fare declines rapidly. I have never noticed much difference in striped bass myself, but I know a lot of folks who vastly prefer a 29-incher to a bigger fish. In any case, while it is not uncommon for a smaller fish to be preferable nowhere in my experience is the difference as drastic as it is with bluefish. Fileting a two-pound bluefish reveals nice firm meat with a pinkish hue and very little dark meat. As they get larger, their flesh gets softer and greyer, and a higher percentage of it is dark meat. The little ones are tasty enough that a few of the captains and mates I know will take a couple two or three pounders home for dinner on occasion, preferring it to even the highly sought-after culinary prize, the striped bass.

Until I catch the little bluefish, I will be in the position of literally fishing for food on the table, which, perhaps ironically, is something of a rarity for me. The truth is that I do not much care for fish. After a long day on the water, or any day for that matter, I prefer steak, pasta, or any number of other options. I love seafood, lobsters, oysters, shrimp, really shellfish of all kinds, calamari and octopus, crab. I tried sea urchin and loved it. I am not a timid eater. With the notable exception of tuna and the occasional ceviche, I just do not really care for most of the fish I catch. I have eaten quite a bit of it, probably a lot more than a lot of people who actually like it, due in part to the fact that in my younger days I killed quite a few fish mostly to prove that I could, and I have always tried to abide the rule that if I kill something I have to eat it.

I was fishing the bonita bar with Bill Palmer a couple years ago, and after releasing a bunch of them, I commented off hand that it sure would be great if we could catch cows and go home from fishing trips with big brimming bags of ribeyes, to which he agreed wholeheartedly. That is a nice delicious thought, but if causes you to wonder if that were the case, would I then go home desirous of fish for dinner? Most sportfishing captains that I know of do not go home every night, or even weekly with some striped bass or bluefish. Who wants to go home and eat it after working with it all day? On the other hand, after a successful duck or deer hunt I regard the culinary reward as outstanding, so perhaps it is really just my personal taste rather than a distaste bred from familiarity.

While considering the relationship between my diet and my fishing, I believe there is much to be gained by separating them as completely as possible. Certainly, in the beginning fishing was about survival: catching a fish for the purpose of killing it, and eating it. But we have come a long way from that. For most experienced anglers these days, taking dinner home from a fishing trip is certainly not the priority and at times it is not even a consideration. Many of the world's most sought after fish, billfish, bonefish, and tarpon, are targeted overwhelmingly with the purpose of letting them go. My freshwater experience is limited, and my trout experience even more so, but the literature of the sport suggests that killing a trout, especially a big one, is seldom endorsed. For the experienced angler, coming home empty handed is often the case; dinner is seldom a barometer of success.

However, at the entry level and for much of the non-angling public, fishing still seems to be about coming home with dinner. I suppose this is natural if most of your exposure to fish comes from menus and supermarkets. While it may be natural to associate fishing with bringing home dinner, for the beginning angler, I recommend trying to distance yourself from that thinking as quickly and completely as possible. The joys of angling found in the hunt and pursuit of the fish, the tempting, the fighting, and ultimately subduing the fish are more than satisfactory. Adding a release to the end of it is also rewarding. In my mind's eye right now I can picture a number of truly large and beautiful fish swimming away after being released, but I am having trouble conjuring a remembrance of a taste or sight of one that made it to the table.

In the charter boat business many of the customers are interested in taking home dinner. It is especially prevalent with the walk-up crowd on Straight Wharf. It seems that fishing trips to Alaska where stocking the freezer is apparently a priority have permeated the consciousness of the whole country. Everybody in America seems to have a cousin, an uncle, a neighbor, a friend, or a friend of a friend who went fishing in Alaska and had the fish steaked or fileted, packed, frozen, and shipped home. Many people have benefitted from these trips as the recipient of a frozen chunk of salmon or halibut once the angler returned home and received their package only to realize the limitations of their own freezer space. The by-product of this is that sportfishing guides nationwide are continuously peppered with questions from tourists about packing and shipping home their catch. I am not sure how or why this is a good option in Alaska; perhaps because you can expect to catch quite a lot of tasty fish, but nowhere else in America is this a good or cost effective option. In fact, freezing and shipping your catch eliminates the only good reason I see to be preoccupied with catching something in order to eat, which is freshness really does matter with seafood, and there is something to be said for catching a fish and eating it the same day.

Somebody close to every charter boat dock in America could probably make a buck or two packing and shipping fish, though it would be a distasteful joke on tourists, hugely insensitive to both the fish populations and the human palette. Thankfully, in most places I am familiar with, that is not the case. I would also venture a guess that it is not due to the genuine good will toward tourists or deference to healthy fish populations. I would guess the only reason that this packing and shipping is not common is because of the exorbitant rates to pack and ship something quickly, and for folks who view a freezer full of fish as nicely defraying the cost of their fishing trip, shipping prices make their local fish market, chicken, or beef seem like excellent alternatives.

Then there is the crowd that wants to catch dinner and they are willing to sacrifice good fishing to do it. I have nothing against catching dinner. I think going out, catching yourself a fish, preparing it lovingly, and eating it is a top-notch way to spend your day. With the current trends of organic food, emphasis on local food sources, farm-to-table freshness, and general pop culture foodieness, I think that catching and cooking dinner has become a very hip thing to do and I am fine with that. What I caution against is the meal becoming the primary goal of the fishing rather than a pleasant ancillary benefit that should be discarded without much of a second thought.

The difference is perhaps subtle to the non-angler, but I will illustrate how it usually plays out in Nantucket. Even at the height of summer, striped bass are probably available (even on light tackle) in the rips east of the island, but they are not supposed to be targeted, and certainly not kept. This is due to a federal management policy that is just plain stupid, but delving into the minutia of that here is too depressing. The long and the short of it is that fishing for striped bass is not allowed in some of the best, most consistent striped bass fishing spots in the world, and if you are not willing to break the law, you have to look elsewhere for a striped bass dinner.

Sankaty is probably the next best bet, but many days it is a far cry. During the summer months, big bluefish are present, plentiful, and hungry, while striped bass, if they are present, will almost certainly be somewhat lethargic, exhibit some reticence to eating, and generally be keeping a low profile. Targeting the bluefish with a spinning rod or a fly rod could lead to a lot of reel screaming excitement. Often the fish are tailing and daisy chaining, making sight fishing a real possibility. The fish are almost exclusively large, over eight pounds with plenty of fish eclipsing the ten pound mark. And despite the general availability of the bluefish, most of the boats there, both charter and private, will be trolling wire lines in search of striped bass. The fact that striped bass are a few steps above the bluefish in terms of gamefish glamorousness is to some degree responsible for it being the predominant target, but certainly some of it has to do with their relative food value as well.

While I lack the familiarity with the details, I am sure that similar scenarios play out all over the world. On trips when the fishing should be just about the fishing, judgment is clouded with thoughts of dinner and fun is missed out on. Unfortunately, it is probably the inexperienced angler who makes the mistake most, and also the inexperienced angler who would benefit most from the separation of fish and plate.

Make no mistake, I am not against fish for dinner, especially when it is caught in an environmentally responsible way. Tomorrow, I will be on the lookout for a little bluefish to feed my family, a short return to subsistence fishing. I really appreciate the culinary reward of a successful bluefin trip. I really love spicy conch chowder of the variety common in the Bahamas and South Florida. I betrayed my New England roots that require chowder to be of a cream base, and made a version of the spicy red chowder with striped bass instead of conch, and the memory of that has me planning on bringing home a striper next time I have the chance. The foodie in me loves the idea of catching a few black sea bass and cooking them whole. Maybe I will stuff them with lobster, scallops or crab, that way I will still enjoy dinner even after the first couple bites when I remember I do not particularly like fish. Or maybe a delicious black sea bass prepared in such a way will make a convert of me.

Even with all these potentially tasty dishes in my mind, the idea of catching a bonefish or a billfish or even a big bluefish appeals to me more, and fun will remain the main goal of my fishing. If you are fishing for fun, that doesn't mean you may not get dinner too, it will just help align your priorities.

8

In Pursuit of Glory

*Thoughts on the Lameness of Modern Professional
Sports, The Hazard of Tournament Fishing, and my Total
Incapability to do anything in Moderation*

I am writing this during the Super Bowl in which the
Ravens are playing the 49er's, and which I am not watching.
Years ago, I never would have predicted that I would miss a
Superbowl, and certainly not to do something as mundane as get
some writing done. I really love football. It is probably my
favorite sport, and if there were a touch-football game I could
take part in right now, I would be out the door without a second
thought. I would even consider getting into a full-pads, full
contact game, but I may not be in shape for that, and I would
have to lie to my wife about it. She is apprehensive about any
continued athletics, especially since a broken finger that required
surgery from a flag football game a couple years ago and the
nastiest black eye of my life more recently from a fly ball I lost in
the sun during a baseball game. Despite my love of football,
here I sit, writing, while the biggest football game of the year is
being played.

I am not watching for a number of reasons, one being
that I do not care about the Ravens or 49er's. I also do not care

about the commercials, though I did watch the allegedly racist Volkswagon commercial on the internet, and found it funny and inoffensive. I am glad Jamaica issued an official statement saying they like it.

Mostly, I am not watching because I have given up professional sports fandom all together. From the time I started to understand sports until a couple years ago, I was a fairly serious Patriots and Red Sox fan. I was never their biggest fan, New England having plenty of over the top fanatics, but I was certainly enthusiastic. I seldom if ever missed a Patriots game and I owned both a Drew Bledsoe and Tom Brady jersey. My enthusiasm for the Red Sox tended to wane a little bit in mid-summer (whose doesn't during a 162 game season? certainly not most players) but I was excited by the start of baseball in the spring and I was riveted by the post-season. I was involved and invested to the point that at times I unraveled into a total emotional wreck (game seven of the 2003 ALCS being a particular low point). But over time my fan experience became unsatisfactory, and eventually, I swore it off altogether.

The first problem is players switching teams. It is a bigger problem with baseball than with football, but the problem persists in both. You get attached to a guy, start liking him, rooting for him, and the next thing you know, he is gone. I saw Roger Clemens throw a one-hitter with my Dad on our first trip to Fenway together. What is a fan to do when he departs for Toronto and then the Yankees? Obviously, it has gotten much worse since then. Nomar Garciaparra was traded in the midst of the World Series season after being the backbone of the whole team for years, Pedro Martinez departed shortly afterward, Kevin Millar, fan and clubhouse favorite was forced to find a new team, and perhaps the worst blow, Johnny Damon departed for the Yankees.

The opposite is true as well and you can't become too comfortable disliking players. As far as I can tell, pretty much everybody in the world dislikes Alex Rodriguez. But when it was clear he was leaving the Rangers, everybody wanted him on their team and started singing his praises. When he went to New York rather than Boston, we were free to dislike him again.

While football is not as bad, there are plenty of departures. Long-time Patriots Mike Vrabel, Lawyer Milloy, and Ty Law had to finish their careers elsewhere. Willie McGinest, a personal favorite of mine, was shipped off. The circumstances in which Drew Bledsoe departed were understandable, but the end result was still the same: a very classy guy and somebody you could root for leaving the team. Deon Branch seems to be in a revolving door with the Patriots, and the list goes on. I do not mean to suggest that I know better than Bill Belichick who should stay and who should go. On the contrary, I think it is fairly hard to question anything the man does regarding football. He should listen to me about football as soon as I should listen to him about fishing (Belichick summers on Nantucket and I often see him out in his boat, *Five Rings*, but from what I have observed, his genius for scheming and play calling does not extend to his choice of lures and fishing spots). His job is to win football games, and he has proven extremely good at it, but what is the cost of the winning? What if Tom Brady loses a little touch or a little accuracy in a few years? Will he go the way of Vrabel, McGinist, and Bledsoe before him and be traded or released, moving off to a second-rate NFL team pinning their hopes to whatever magic is left in the arm of the perhaps the greatest quarterback to play the game? Loyal Patriots fans are supposed to say farewell Tom and embrace the new guy, whom they know nothing about, and who in all likelihood has absolutely no ties to New England. Frankly, I would find it more appealing to root for an aging bunch of underdogs with whom I had grown familiar trying to win one more championship than embrace a bunch of new faces every year no matter how good they are.

I do not blame the players, why shouldn't they go to the highest bidder? And I do not begrudge them their huge salaries: people are making huge amounts of money off their hard work and ability, why should it be predominantly rich old white men and not themselves? But regardless of who is to blame, and whether an equitable alternative is out there, the constant movement is not good.

In the midst of the departures of familiar players and the arrival of new ones, allegiance to whom is withheld a little more each time because I am unsure of when they will depart, the question of what exactly I was rooting for became difficult to answer. I contemplated the question and the answers I came to were not appealing.

The players are the logical choice. I once rooted for the players, but that does not work anymore because many are not around long enough. I am incapable of switching allegiances quickly based on the whims of coaches and sports executives. Add the fact that even if I was still comfortable rooting for the players, in many cases overlooking both unsportsmanlike behavior on the field and off-the-field faux pas became increasingly difficult to justify. I was forced to question whether some of these guys were deserving of my support.

And if I am not rooting for the players, am I rooting for the coach? That doesn't work because they are on the move as often as the players. Terry Francona led the Red Sox to their first World Series in eighty-six years, overcoming not only the Yankees and the best of National League but a longstanding mystical curse, then wins it again, only to be shuffled out shortly thereafter.

I could not root for the players, and I couldn't root for the coach or manager (and even if I could, would that be very exciting). The next answer, and perhaps the obvious one, was that I was rooting for my "home team." I was a Boston fan. Certainly, the Red Sox are Boston. The Patriots are Boston.

And I was only a casual basketball fan, and never a hockey fan, but the Celtics and Bruins are Boston. The teams are embedded into the region's persona as much as the American Revolution, the lobsters, and the accent put together. But what makes this so? It certainly is not that the Patriots and Red Sox are made up of the greatest athletes New England has to offer. I am not watching guys who I once played against in high school. If I was, I could probably get behind them. But this is nothing new, the players have not been from Boston or New England for quite some time. Ted Williams was a California boy, Larry Bird from Indiana, and Bobby Orr from Ontario. Despite their birth taking place elsewhere, it at least seems that Boston or New England became a kind of adopted hometown to them more so than it does for many players today. The concept of a "home team" has become too muddled, and in my search for what I was rooting for, I moved on.

Do I root for the Kraft family and John Henry and whoever else owns the Red Sox? I could probably get into it if they were my buddies and I could advise them on trades and things, but I have no relationship with them and I find it impossible to get behind them. Robert Kraft seems like a hell of a guy, but I believe his fortune was made largely in paper and real estate development and that raises some red flags to an environmentalist like me. Even if I give him the benefit of the doubt as a person, I am not going to devote my Sundays to monitor his fortunes as an owner. And what would I do if he sold the team?

Having unfortunately run out of options, I was forced to make the conclusion that essentially, I was rooting for a uniform or a team name. Devoting the kind of time and energy that I devoted to sports, and realizing that all I was rooting for was a name or a uniform did not sit well with me. What if the entire rosters of the Red Sox and Yankees switched uniforms before game seven of an ALCS? Who would people root for? Perhaps this a ridiculous question, but what if a few of them switched uniforms before the season, a few more halfway through the season, and it seemed likely a few more would switch after the season? Now it sounds like reality, and the ridiculous part becomes not the uniform switching, but why I cared so much for the fate of my chosen uniform.

The recent success of both the Red Sox and Patriots is a significant factor in my giving up fandom. If the Red Sox had not won the World Series, or if the Patriots had not won the Superbowl, I would probably still be a fan. I spent my youth and a chunk of my early adulthood waiting. I spent innumerable hours listening to the radio, watching television, listening to predictions, keeping up with offseason trades, etc., all the while waiting and hoping that the Red Sox would win a World Series and the Patriots would win a Superbowl. A significant portion of my life was spent waiting and hoping. Then they did it. And then they did it again, and for the Patriots, again. I was happy, but ultimately it was a tremendous letdown. After all that time waiting and wishing and hoping, my life didn't change at all after they won. Honestly, I do not know how I anticipated that my life would change. I was not expecting a World Series bonus check from the Red Sox for my years of dedicated rooting, and I was not surprised when the Patriots failed to send me a Superbowl ring (or three). I was not ridiculous enough to believe I would receive anything tangible, but I suppose I did expect something intangible. When you spend a significant portion of your life waiting and wanting something, and then it happens, shouldn't your life change somehow? If it doesn't, what the hell was all the waiting and wishing for? And nothing happened. I suppose I wanted some kind of happiness or inner peace. I may have thought I would find some kind of eternal comfort knowing that my teams were once World Champions, and I now know that, but it has brought me no lasting happiness. I got no sense of accomplishment from the entire thing, despite the fact that I often yelled loudly at the television set during their games (much to my mother's chagrin).

What I did get was a reprieve from the waiting and hoping. Now I know what it is like for your team to win the Superbowl and I know what it is like for your team to win the World Series, and I know, at least for me, it is not worth it because in the end it is a just a bunch of guys I don't know, and who might be gone soon, and who may or may not be good people, wearing the uniform I have pledged allegiance to. And perhaps I should be thankful for that, because entire generations of Red Sox fans were not that lucky. In about 2002, I was at the funeral of a man who had passed in his seventies after a full life. I was standing within earshot of two of his pals, and one said to the other one, "He never got to see the Sox win one," at which point I almost broke down totally. It was by far the saddest thing I heard all day. Now, unlike that poor bastard, at least I can live my life knowing what it feels like when the Red Sox win the World Series. But it seems to me that the hope of victory was more fulfilling and more sustaining than the actual victory, and perhaps if that man had lived to see the Sox win, it would have only led to a disturbing fan-faith crisis late in life.

My questions regarding my own fandom came to the forefront when they lost. If the Patriots or Red Sox lost a game, especially a big game, my mood would be negatively affected. I would be irritable and inconsolable. Now, not only did my life not improve at all when a bunch of guys I didn't know won World Championships, my life was measurably worse when they did not win. The same factors that prohibited me from enjoying their wins (I threw no touchdowns, made no tackles, got no hits, stole no bases) did not seem to console me when they lost (I did not let up any hits, commit any errors, miss any tackles or throw any interceptions).

Even in the face of these growing questions, my devotion eroding at least in my mind if not through my actions, I continued to watch. Patriots and Red Sox fandom was not something that would be swept away easily. One day, I was with my buddies, and it was an absolutely beautiful day in late September. We were together to watch the Patriots, but looking outside, we wondered whether the time would be better spent outdoors. Eventually, after much debate, we decided the time was better spent outdoors and we went fishing. We enjoyed the afternoon immensely, catching bluefish at Great Point, and I couldn't even believe that we had considering staying on the couch. Perhaps catching a bluefish is not as much as an accomplishment as winning a Superbowl, but it is *my* accomplishment, and that was the last straw. I decided to give it up, and I have not been a fan since. I figured when I decided to give it up, that it would not last and I would still plant myself on the couch for most Patriots game, but that has not been the case. When you like to hunt and fish as much as I do, the extra time is nice. Actually going fishing, logging some family time, or taking care of things in order to hunt and fish more during the week all proved more worthwhile than sitting on the couch eating an obscene amount of junk food and yelling at the television.

I watched the Superbowl last year, figuring that the rest of America watches it, even the non-fans, so I might as well take it in. I was disappointed the Patriots lost, but I was happy that I wasn't emotionally invested in the entire thing. I caught a few minutes of a game that was on at a birthday party a couple weeks ago, and it seemed a flag was thrown every time somebody got hit. It crossed my mind that if I hadn't already given up watching the game, all the flags could have done it. I understand player safety is an important issue, and I don't like to see a lot of guys getting a lot of concussions, but the flags were too frequent and the penalties too significant to the outcome to make it much good to watch. Luckily, these are not concerns I have anymore.

I have not watched a Red Sox game in several years and the last Patriots Superbowl was the last NFL game I watched. I am very happy with the results, having deduced that fandom was providing far more grief than joy and also taking up a tremendous amount of time. Given my success with giving up fandom, and other things, I am considering giving up tournament fishing.

The idea of giving up tournament fishing altogether occurred to me during the second day of a two-day tournament in which we were unsuccessful in catching the fish we needed to win the tournament. Mike and I were not happy. We had a great day one, and we were extremely well positioned along with only one or two other boats to win, but we did not catch the right fish on day two to stay in contention.

However, when we looked back on the day, it had been a fine day on the water. The weather was great, and our anglers had enjoyed themselves immensely. Perhaps most ironically, the fishing had been pretty good. We had caught false albacore, bluefish, and striped bass, including a beautiful forty-inch fish that tore off an impressive amount of line from a spinning rod. But despite having caught plenty of fish and a three-species slam, we knew we didn't have a chance at first place because the right angler had not caught the right fish using the right methods. The tournament was the Nantucket Slam, and the rules are fairly complex. Different point values are associated with different methods of fishing, and large bonus points come into play when an angler releases three or more species. While we had caught fish, our angler who had the most false albacore didn't catch the striped bass, and our angler with the striped bass needed more albacore, and we couldn't get striped bass without trolling while all our albacore had been casting, and so on, with the result being we were not in contention for "Overall Grand Champion" title, which had been our goal (salt would be rubbed in the wound at the awards when we learned we also missed the "Most False Albacore" award by a single fish, and the "Biggest Striped Bass" award by a half an inch).

This may sound like an indictment of the tournament, whereby a great day fishing can somehow be lost in the minutia of rules, but that is not the case at all. In fact, I am genuinely fond of the tournament rules and points system. The Nantucket Slam is a *Redbone Series* tournament, and in the original *Redbone* anglers have to target both bonefish and redfish, both fish being accessible from Islamorada, but generally not found in the same areas. It is a fun and interesting concept, and rewarding versatility as well as testing the limits of the anglers and captains is a good tournament goal. The Nantucket Slam embraces the same concept, and to have a chance at being the Grand Champion angler, you have got to rack up some "Slam" bonus points which come each time you put three species in the boat, with even greater bonus points if you can add the fourth (striped bass, bluefish, bonito and false albacore being the four tournament species). I like the format and I like the set-up, and I think they do an excellent job of awarding points in an equitable fashion which is not easy given the fact that you have people trolling from big sportfishers and others fly casting from skiffs all in the same tournament. It is certainly not the Nantucket Slam that I find fault with, but with some aspects of tournament fishing in general.

For instance, early on day two we arrived to a rip where I hoped to find striped bass. There were some albies popping up around the rip and we caught one fairly quickly. But instead of enjoying the albie action, we tried the edge of the rip itself for stripers, and found none, and shortly thereafter, made our way to another rip, even though the albies were still popping up. We had already caught many albies on day one of the tournament, and on day two we needed stripers to amass the critical bonus points, and so we ran away from the busting albies, in search of stripers, a search that was marginally successful yet unfulfilling.

One potential answer to this, of course, is to say to hell with bonus points and tournament standings and just have a fun day bending rods; at the end of fishing just let the points fall where they may. My anglers seem to take that approach, with happiness and contentment resulting from their tournament experience. They were pleased as punch to have caught plenty of fish over the two days, happy as clams to have got a few nice stripers during what by all accounts was lackluster striper fishing, and generally jovial about the whole thing. There may be something to this, and it is certainly a possibility, but it runs a little against my grain. This moderate approach may work where professional sports are concerned as well. Why not take in the occasional game? I like watching football and baseball. I like some of the athletes; some of them are good guys who have made New England their adoptive hometown. But it is not in the cards for me.

I tend to be an all or nothing type person. If I am going to do something, I tend to do it all the way (or perhaps, as my wife may argue, even go overboard). I find it virtually impossible to cook a simple dinner. If I set out to make pasta and sauce, I may even start with the plan to boil some noodles, cover them with a jarred sauce and eat. Then I think why eat jarred sauce when a homemade sauce would be much better and why not add a meat, perhaps some meatballs. Frozen meatballs are tolerable, but I have a great recipe for homemade meatballs that I have been perfecting for a couple years, and I really would prefer those, and if I am making meatballs, it will not be much more trouble to brown some sausages, and as long as I am browning sausage, I might as well brown and add a small pork butt to the sauce. Add garlic bread, freshly chopped parsley and fresh parmesan (because why go to all the trouble and then skimp on the details?) and before you know it, one of the simplest dinners available, pasta and sauce, has become an all day production of a complex Italian Sunday gravy that has dirtied most of the dishes and all of the cutlery in the kitchen. Either that or I forget the whole thing and order take out. Most of the time, I classify this behavior under the favorable heading of 'anything worth doing is worth doing right,' but I suppose that it would also be possible to classify my behavior as a total incapability to do anything in moderation.

The casual approach, to tournament fishing or fandom, is probably not in the cards. During the Superbowl last year, with every rational thought in my brain telling me that I was better off not being emotionally tied to the outcome of the game, I had the urge to yell at the television. My heart still dropped when the sure-handed Wes Welker dropped the pass that would have iced the game, and my mood was probably negatively affected when the Patriots lost, though only slightly as compared to past seasons of devoted fandom.

It is difficult for me to enter a tournament and then fish it casually. If I am in it, then I want to win it. I do not go out there with a few rods, ready to take some casts and troll around and see what happens. I want at least thirty rods and reels at the ready, with a variety of lures, rigged in triplicate so if one lure and method are successful the other anglers can immediately switch over without any wasted time spent re-rigging.

I cannot put my finger on why, but it also seems like a further indictment of me that the Nantucket Slam is a wonderful charity tournament to benefit the Cystic Fibrosis Foundation. In past years the overall grand champion has been awarded either a poster or a cutting board, both of which are very nice, but both of which could be purchased for a tiny fraction of the fuel cost associated with fishing two days. Perhaps this is to my credit. I am a competitor and my will to win is not greed-driven, though I may just crave the win for vanity and pride, and that isn't too much better than greed, and in any case, it is vaguely unsettling.

Erik Passanante and I also fished a one-day Nantucket Anglers' Club Bluefin Tuna tournament in 2012, also with disappointing results that make me question tournament fishing. On our way to the spot we had planned to fish, we came across busting fish. Normally, it would have been a welcome stroke of luck, but under the circumstances, it presented us with a number of ethical and moral dilemmas. The time was about 4:45AM, and the lines-in time for the tournament was 5:00AM. The stakes of the ethical questions were high because of the nature of bluefin fishing. Under federal regulations we were allowed only one fish that day, and bluefin often bite best in the early morning. If we put the lines in the water and caught a fish, would we release it and try for another fish within the tournament time frame? Would we kill it with the idea that a fish in the boat makes the day a success, even if it was not a fish we could weigh in the tournament? Of course, putting the lines in right away, catching a fish, keeping it, and weighing it, was a distinct possibility. Nobody was near us and even if there were boats around it was thick fog. The tournament committee does not have eyes twenty-five miles east of Nantucket, and nobody would have given it a second thought if we said we caught the fish at 5:15 rather than 4:45. While certainly a tempting solution, it was not one I considered. If I fish a tournament, I want to fish it all-out, and if rules are laid out for the tournament, they should be followed. I know plenty of guys who take some liberties with certain fishing regulations. I think certain fishing regulations are ridiculous, and from time to time, I have chosen to interpret some of them loosely (or disregard them totally) myself. It is not that I am a total stickler for the rules, or too much of chicken-shit to make an occasional departure from the law, it is that I believe tournament fishermen should hold themselves to a high standard of compliance. If somebody was caught breaking a law, I would not necessarily think less of them, especially if their crime was not detrimental to the environment or the law they were breaking was a bad one, but if somebody cheated in a tournament, I would certainly think less of them. Tournaments are signed up for voluntarily, and if you are not going to follow the tournament rules you never should have signed up, whereas we can not opt out of laws, even bad ones. I knew that if we took some liberties with the lines-in time we would not be caught, but I also knew any financial gain or joy I derived from winning the tournament would be totally eclipsed by a heavy conscience.

In any case, we dilly-dallied getting the lines out, and no moral issues needed further contemplation because we did not get a bite before five, nor after five. The busting fish went down right before five, and we went the day without a fish. Who knows if we would have gotten a fish if not forced to wrestle with ethics, but that is not really the point. The point is, that busting bluefin, like the busting albies in the Nantucket Slam, should have been targeted immediately and zealously. Our good fortune as anglers to find feeding fish on surface should have been recognized and celebrated, and instead, due to the various circumstances involved in tournament fishing, other factors were considered.

The last recent incident that brings me to consider the merits of tournament fishing is that this fall, during world-class albie fishing, I was considering striper fishing. I had already weighed in a fly-rod albacore for the Inshore Classic, and I needed to weigh in a fly rod striper if I was to have a chance at winning the boat fly rod division. The albie fishing was off-the-charts good, and for the second year in a row, fall striped bass fishing was between bad and nonexistent. But instead of taking what was available, and fishing for what was biting, sage advice I often give, I was thinking about where to find a striped bass, preferably a large one, that would eat a fly. If not for my participation in a tournament, I would have been more than content to focus on the obliging albies.

Given my recent qualms with tournament fishing, I am now considering giving it up altogether. I have given up quite a few things in addition to fandom over the last six years or so, and in nearly every case, my life has improved substantially as a result. Among the things I have given up are booze, drugs, cigarettes, potato chips, and golf. Drinking was the hardest thing to give up, but it also had the biggest positive impact. As you can imagine, my characteristic aversion to moderation was a much bigger problem when pertaining to alcohol than to fandom, tournament fishing and pasta dinners. Cigarettes were also a tough one, probably because fishing is very conducive to smoking, especially offshore trolling. You are simultaneously very tense and on edge, looking for fish, thinking about fish, wondering if they will rise and bite, while at the same time you are very bored, looking at the endless ocean, watching your lures, waiting and waiting and waiting for a fish bite. This bizarre combination of extreme boredom and extreme tension lends itself very well to heavy smoking, and I would suspect that in a per capita analysis of smoking by career, that offshore captains and mates have one of the highest rates of smoking. I gave up golf for no other reason than I felt I was spreading myself too thin over a number of leisure activities. The amount of time I spend fishing with clients, combined with amount of time I spend fishing without clients, combined with the various responsibilities of family life, leaves precious little time for an occasional tennis game, much less eighteen holes. And golf is not a game that rewards the occasional duffer. Being good at golf is no easy task, and to do it when you are not much good at it results in more frustration than fun, much like fly fishing, and so it was more an issue of time than of me having to give it up. If I played a few holes tomorrow for instance, it would probably not effect my life much going forward, but instead if I had a couple cocktails, I would likely encounter serious consequences sooner rather than later.

Potato chips I claim to have given up, but there are occasional lapses in that one. That was just a matter of trying keep my weight in check, the fact that I am prone to eating the entire bag, and that while I do enjoy potato chips, I felt I could give them up, unlike steak and pasta, which probably have a similar effect on my weight, but will remain in my diet for the foreseeable future.

Given my success at giving things up and the subsequent improvement in my life, I wonder what other things I can shed to lead a more fulfilling and content life. However, the business of giving things up could go too far. The booze, drugs and cigarettes were obvious choices, fandom has proved successful, but the tournament fishing? Who knows what it may lead to after that? If I keep giving things up, it could lead to a kind of vegen, celibate, monastic existence, and that is certainly not what I am looking for. When I gave up the booze and drugs I feared I may be mistaken for some kind of straight-laced conservative ninny, so I have at times let my hair grow, I listen to the Grateful Dead and Bob Marley even more than I did when I was doing drugs, invested in environmental bumper stickers, and just in general tried to make it known that while my social life is fairly sedate, my stance on politics and life remain liberal.

Tournament fishing is certainly not all bad. I am generally a competitive bastard, and competing is a good way to get life juices flowing. On fishing trips among friends I generally organize a tournament of sorts. Nothing formal, but a few bucks tossed into the pot and awarded to a myriad of categories. These tournaments are responsible for squeezing even more joy out of most fishing trips. A few of these trips have been to Pine Island, FL, and in such a locale, with a wide variety of species, the categories can get numerous. Our tournaments will include biggest redfish, biggest snook, biggest fish, most redfish and snook, most fish, species count and best raccoon eyes, awarded the angler with the most drastic sunglasses-tan-line, which I maintain is an extremely sexy look. While some fish don't count in our tournaments (the slimy and annoying catfish being an example) they are not restricted to only the glamour species either; a ladyfish or a little grouper can be the difference in the species count, which adds an interesting element to the angling. The stakes, both in terms of actual monetary value and bragging rights, are pretty small but there is a general air of enthusiasm about the whole thing.

I am not ready to abandon tournament fishing, but it is something to keep an eye on. Anything that has the potential to put a negative spin on a good day of fishing is suspect, and tournaments certainly have the capability to do that. But they are fun. In fact, part of me looks forward to the next Nantucket Slam already. I like the atmosphere, I like hanging around talking fishing with all the anglers and guides, I like the anticipation of having just a little something extra on the line during a day of fishing. Maybe next year if faced with the same circumstances I will just stay put and have a blast catching albies, or maybe I will still chase elusive stripers. Either way, the stakes will be just a little higher than normal and that is not necessarily something to avoid. Someday, when time and money permit, perhaps I will head south and fish a *Redbone* as an angler, which I would get a real kick out of.

As opposed to the fandom of professional sports, the accomplishments of tournament fishing are *my* accomplishments. My tournament victories have been followed by real and deserved joy. While I never caught a touchdown from Tom Brady in a Superbowl or hit a changeup over the Green Monster in the fall classic, I have taken my angler to the right spots at the right times with the right lure and won the Nantucket Slam, I have tied a pretty enough fly and made a long enough cast to catch tournament winning fly rod albacore. And in the end, that is probably enough. I am willing to put a little more on the line, I am willing to risk a potentially good day of fishing for a shot at tournament glory, because it will be my glory.

In Pursuit of Enough
To Fly Fish or Not to Fly Fish

When the incoming tide coincides with sunrise in August, and my schedule allows, I will get up early and go fish the bonito bar. The sun rises early in August, but it is not quite as brutal as trying to beat the sun to the water in June. Sometimes Mike will accompany me. My Uncle Bob is usually willing, and clients Bill Palmer and Erik Passanante are with me at times, but fishing with those guys is a lot more like fishing with a friend than a customer. I intend to start taking Liz with me again at some point, and sometimes I will go by myself. If conditions are right and the ocean is smooth enough, upon arrival I will hear the bait. In a couple hours the light will be on the water enough to be able to look in and see the big bait balls, but not yet. You cannot see them at dawn, but the sand eels are there, and they will be flipping around on the surface enough, and in such numbers, that it will be audible. The whole scene looks and feels fishy, and perhaps along with the effervescence of the sand eels, I will even witness or perceive signs of the larger predators, a splash here or a boil there. To this point, I could not have asked for better conditions.

I will have a spinning rod with braided line, a 25lbs. fluorocarbon leader, and a Yo-Zuri Crystal Minnow (probably more than one actually), and an eight-weight with a flashy bonito bunny (and to be honest, maybe more than one fly rod too). A couple years ago they would have all been rigged with precision the night before in a state of happy anticipation, but more likely these days they are left rigged from the day before when I rushed home to assist Liz with Chick after a day of fishing with clients.

I will be in one of my favorite spots on earth, at the absolute best time of day, with perfect conditions, and I will be faced with a difficult and daunting question. Do I pick up the spinning rod or the fly rod? And it is not just a bonito bar problem. One of the biggest questions I face as an angler, no matter where I find myself fishing, is to fly fish, or not to fly fish. It is pretty rare these days that I do not have both kinds of tackle with me, and upon arrival at my chosen spot I must decide which to pick up. It is a practical question, addressed on a cast-by-cast basis when on the water, and it is a philosophical question, contemplated for long hours in the off-season. Sometimes the question is already answered by the circumstances it is posed under: the practical, cast-by-cast decision in the height of the fishing season is to pick up a spinning rod, while off-season daydreaming and contemplation corresponds much better to the fly rod.

To be sure, fly fishing played a large role in my formative fishing years, changing from a kid who fished to a young man who lived for fishing. It was the mid-nineties, and fly fishing was new, at least to most Northeast saltwater folks, and it carried an electric vibe. The venerable Bill Fisher Tackle, then the back part of Bill Pew's house on New Lane, started dedicating about half its inventory to fly tackle, and even had a substantial section devoted to tying materials. On a few occasions, I met with a few men, uniformly older but anywhere from twenty-something to seventy, and we were the fledgling Nantucket Fly Fishing Club, or something like that. I forget the name, but we did have one all-night bass tournament and got

110

Lefty Kreh to come to the island and give casting lessons. The club sort of faded into the background, most of the members being members of the Angler's Club anyway and realizing that running another club would probably cut into their fishing time, but the point is, it was an exciting time in fly fishing.

I read and re-read Nick Curcione's *Orvis Guide to Saltwater Fly Fishing*. I got the casting lesson from Lefty Kreh. I had a vice, bucktails, and threads set up next to my weight-lifting bench in the basement. I spent many afternoons lifting weights in anticipation of football season and then tying flies in anticipation of fishing season. The fly-tying habit stuck; a large portion of my basement is still dedicated to vices, hooks, threads, bucktails, various forms of tinsel, and more fly tying knickknacks and doo-dads than any non-angler would believe, but the last time I lifted a weight was high school.

At a time in my life when girls, sports, general misbehavior and any number of other things were competing with fishing for my attention, fly fishing added a new and exciting attraction to boating with my Dad. It wasn't always harmonious. I often blamed him for positioning the boat poorly in relation to the schools of bluefish we would chase, though in retrospect my shortcomings with a fly rod were probably responsible for most of the missed opportunities. My father probably wondered why the hell I didn't just catch one on a spinning rod with a popper, but perhaps not. He was content with boat rides, and tallying many bluefish releases did not seem a priority. Nevertheless, it was time with my father and time on the water, which, even if a portion of it is spent mad at each other, it was far more wholesome and life affirming than any number of other things I may have been doing. Even in those days, when the fly rod added a new and exciting element, I never became a fly fisherman exclusively, perhaps preferring to fly fish, but never against casting or even trolling. And then, for a period of a few years, I drifted away from it. Again, never giving it up completely, always owning a fly rod and sometimes using it, but in a mirror image to the years before, much more likely to have a spinning rod in my hand, and many times even, leaving the fly rod at home.

I think, more than anything, this had to do with the fact that I had not caught enough fish yet. In those first years of fly fishing, bluefish were the target, and with a youth of chasing them behind me, for the most part, I had caught enough bluefish. When striped bass started to reappear and then pervade the angling scene, I had not caught enough of them. Wire line was the widely known ticket to Sankaty striped bass, and with the promise of striped bass, I went from one end of the tackle spectrum to the other, many summer days with my father spent jigging wire line instead of casting a fly. On my beach outings, my fly rod was sometimes put in the car, but it usually stayed there, because my best chance for a striper was with a spinning rod.

Then, at eighteen, I started running the *Topspin* out of Straight Wharf. I had a captain's license and plenty of fishing experience, but Straight Wharf was the big leagues and I had a ways to go. Josh Eldridge and Bobby DeCosta had been chartering off Straight Wharf for years before my arrival, and both caught big striped bass with a consistency that I hadn't thought possible, hadn't dreamed of. I spent hours paranoid about their secret spots, secret methods, and at times suspected they possessed some kind of magical fish-conjuring ability. To me, one keeper had previously meant a good day and a cause for happiness and celebration, perhaps not terribly rare, but not a foregone conclusion either. I was thrust into competition with Josh and Bobby, not because I had reached their level, but because of the proximity of our slips. Rather than celebrating the occasional keeper, they consistently caught their limit. Catching striped bass, big ones, and lots of them, became a priority. Fly fishing is seldom the most effective way to catch a fish in saltwater. In those years, my goal was to usually to catch lots of fish, and usually, the fly rod was left untouched.

And the pendulum has swung again in the last few years, and I am back to fly fishing in a big way, though again, not exclusively.

These days, in answering the question, to fly fish or not to fly fish, it usually hinges on the same question: "have I caught enough fish already?" If the answer is yes, then I will fly fish. If the answer is no, I will cast or troll. While the basic question remains the same, it is subject to many variations, and the answer to the question changes all the time as well. For instance, in the spring, when I am found fishing the flats, there is always a fly rod and a spinning rod in the boat, and the question is usually, "have I caught enough fish today?" And usually, if I haven't caught one, my answer is no.

It has been a long winter. I want to see the strike, I want to feel the line come tight, and want to feel the resistance as hold the rod tip high. I want to fight the fish, and I want to get it to the boat and I want to release it, or maybe I even have a friend who wants it for dinner. When I get back on land, I want to be able to answer a truthful yes to whether I caught something. I want to hear the drag scream, and therefore sometimes the question must become, "have I caught a big enough fish today?" Once I have caught one fish, or one big enough fish, my answer usually changes to "yes." The skunk is out of the boat, and I comfortably pick up my fly rod.

Time frame is a critical aspect of the question. Have I caught enough fish today? Have I caught enough fish this year? Have I caught enough fish to this point in my life? If I am looking for my first striper of the season, my fly rod is probably going to be at home, the answer to whether I have caught enough fish this year being a firm no.

In addition to the time frame, the species will also affect the question. In those early days of fly fishing, the question was

113

have I caught enough bluefish, to which the answer was yes, and I fly fished, and when the question was have I caught enough striped bass, the answer was no, and I spin fished and trolled.

These species-based questions are prevalent in my thinking these days. To the question, have I caught enough blue marlin, the answer would be no and the number would be none. Next time I am blue marlin fishing, I will not be doing it with a fly rod. Have I caught enough white marlin- no, so for the foreseeable future I will not throw a fly at one unless I have already tried a scup, an eel, and a ballyhoo. Have I caught enough bluefin tuna? Perhaps, especially school-sized ones, and next time I would like to throw a fly at one. Though, the answer to the question, "have I caught enough bluefin tuna today" will probably be no and the fly rod will stay put away until one fish is in the boat.

To the question "have I caught enough permit?" the answer on most days would be yes.

While I was in law school, a couple friends from college, Paul Jackson and Toph Gorab, flew into Miami for a visit and we all headed to Key West. My Uncle Bob had advised me, when fishing Key West, to charter a versatile center console (of which many are available), on the theory that if the fishing was good offshore, it was accessible, and if fishing was good inshore, that was accessible too, giving you better odds at getting into some good fishing. We fished with Captain Ryon Logan on his 27' Conch. In prior conversations with Ryon, I had told him that sailfish and tuna were our first choice, but if offshore was not good, we were very pleased with tarpon. I talked to him the day before our trip, and he said offshore fishing was slow and tarpon fishing wasn't much better; however, permit had just started spawning on the reef and that it should be good. I had never caught a permit, and agreed that it was the best choice.

The day started with us meeting Ryon and him hustling us onto the boat, and we quickly raced out of the Hurricane Hole

Marina up several Keys to a bait and tackle shop. Ryon explained that that word was out that permit were on the reef, and hence, live crabs (the vastly preferred live bait of permit) were in high demand. Every bait shop from Key West to Key Largo was completely sold out. His friend at the bait and tackle shop a few Keys up was saving him three, but we needed to get there fast before they were discovered. Bait everywhere, but perhaps especially in Florida, is often a numbers game. You want your live wells "blacked out", or filled to capacity, with bait, and often your success on the day will correspond directly with the amount of bait in your well. Our frantic race to a tackle shop for a mere three crabs was bizarre and discomfortingly desperate, but it was not without humor or excitement.

We successfully made it to the store before the crabs were discovered, saving Ryon's friend from being torn limb from limb by crazed permit hunters for holding out on them, but somehow there were only two left. I do not know what happened to the other one; it may have perished, or it may have been traded for a kidney.

In addition to our two crabs, we had a livewell full of shrimp, and Ryon said that while a crab will really excite the fish, they could also be enticed to eat a shrimp if it was put right on their nose.

For those accustomed to, or familiar with, chasing permit on the flats, looking for them over the reef may seem less challenging, less pure, and less rewarding. Certainly, I am of the opinion for the most part that shallower is better. That being said, the day was excellent. The fishing was highly visible, appropriately challenging, and unlike the flats, consistently productive. If I ever get the opportunity to fish the reef for permit again, my answer would be an enthusiastic yes.

Ryon stopped the boat in I believe about thirty or forty feet of water, over patches of reef he deemed appropriate, and we would drift. We stood around the boat, with our spinning rods ready, and looked for permit. Occasionally, you see a fish, or a large group of fish, right along the surface, but as Ryon explained, you were more likely to just see a flash. When the permit turn their side to the sun's rays entering the water, they flash just like a mirror. I had never heard or read about this before, and to be honest, it seemed a little whack-a-do. Peering into thirty or forty feet of water waiting for mysterious "flashes" to cast at did not immediately inspire me with a lot of confidence, but my skepticism didn't last long. Just a few moments into the first drift, I saw a flash, just as advertised. I was the most experienced angler in the group, and I had deferred the crabs to my buddies. I tossed my shrimp in front on the flash, gave it a couple twitches, and then just let it fall as instructed. It was absolutely hammered on the fall, I set the hook, and line flew off my reel. The fish made several impressive runs, and then camped out on the bottom. I would raise it a few feet, only to have it sound again and again. It was a warm day with light winds, and in no time, I was working hard and pouring sweat. As a fish fight, it was more big-game than light tackle, my strength and endurance both being tested. After forty-five minutes, Ryon put the fish in the boat, my first permit, in the forty-pound class. After a quick picture, I released him, and sat down to enjoy a beverage. My permit fishing career, in all likelihood, at least in terms of size, had reached its summit only minutes after it began. They were exciting, terrifying and grueling minutes, but minutes nonetheless.

We continued to have an excellent day. Toph laid one of the crabs out in front of some permit who immediately all raced to inhale it, and shortly thereafter had his first permit. It was a real beauty around twenty pounds, but his sense of proportion was totally out of whack from my fish, and I am not sure he believed it when Ryon assured him that his was in fact a very nice fish.

I hooked another permit, and in the middle of the fight, a hammerhead found us. A brief moment after Ryon saw the big shadow, before I had time to contemplate or execute something like flipping my bail to let the permit make a run for it, the shark had my fish in his mouth. My rod bent double and though it didn't have the speed of a fresh permit, it pulled line off in an unstoppable manner you would expect from a submarine. Its jaws sawed through my fish, and after a little while I was again free to retrieve my permit, unfortunately halved. I was reeling in, the front half of my permit skipped along the surface, and the hammerhead's doral fin popped out behind it. I was determined to save half my permit, and unwilling to feed to the shark anymore, and I started to crank as fast I as I could. The head started to skip faster, but the shark kept coming right for it, keeping pace easily. My permit was almost next to the boat, almost ready to be lifted in with the rod, when the shark lunged for it, caught it and swallowed it, while its momentum carried it into the side of the boat with a crash that made the entire boat shudder. It was an exciting moment.

I forget what happened to our second crab. I think my friend Paul fed it to permit that pulled the hook. Before the end of the day my buddy Toph added a cobia off the back of a ray.

A couple years later I caught another permit, entirely by accident and in the most unlikely way, casting a Mirrolure for redfish and sea trout in Pine Island Sound. Paul and Toph were with me again, and they both looked at the fish and immediately declared it was a permit. It certainly looked like a permit to me, but I was reluctant to declare it such, being that it was the first permit I ever heard of caught on a plug and the first permit I ever heard of being caught in Pine Island Sound. Unfortunately, not only did it eat the Mirrolure, it swallowed it sideways and completely, and was bleeding heavily from the gills. So it was put in the cooler rather than released, and later it was confirmed as a permit by some internet research and local guides Matt Mitchell and Craig Stevens, and eventually grilled by Craig and his family.

Cobia, hammerheads and Mirrolures aside, the answer to whether I have caught enough permit is yes, though I have only caught two. Certainly, the answer to whether I have caught a big enough permit is yes and I will still die a happy man if I never get a permit as big as my first. These days, if I am permit fishing, which is extremely rare but as often as possible, there is no need to make a long or even a short run for precious live crabs. I would like to do it with a fly.

And, where tarpon and bonefish are concerned, I suppose my answer would also be yes, I have caught enough, and now I would like to do it on the fly. It does not escape me though, that perhaps, it is not so much that I have caught enough, it is that I have *not* caught enough on fly. Why did it take two permit for me to reach "enough," whereas I needed to catch about a thousand stripers? Why I am happy to throw a fly at bonefish all day, having in my life caught perhaps two dozen on spinning gear, whereas I have caught perhaps a hundred bluefin and am just now considering throwing a fly at one, and only then probably only when one is already on ice?

Perhaps literature is responsible for many of my views. I am more likely to be content throwing a fly at species traditionally pursued with the fly. Certainly, my strong desire to catch a permit on a fly stems almost entirely from the lofty status that feat is accorded in literature and other angling circles.

Becoming a fly fisherman exclusively is, I suppose, a possibility. Certainly, I would not be the first angler to start with spinning and conventional tackle, then move on to the fly, and eventually not even consider the spinning rod. Many of the literary giants of the sport have taken this path. I believe John Gierach is a fly fisherman exclusively. I am not sure if Tom McGuane objects to picking up a spinning rod these days, but certainly his literature would suggest he is purely fly. Add Nick

Lyons and Robert Traver, a.k.a. John Voelker, and Jim Harrison to the list. The more I read, the more beautiful and seductive fly fishing becomes.

My winter dreams involve flat-calm dawns in the spring, double hauls, and deceivers lightly dropping in front of a cruising pack of stripers, their location given away by a V of nervous water. One eats, I come tight, and fly line then backing disappear as the reel makes its sweet music. It is a gorgeous spring morning, and I am a happy man in paradise. Then, spring actually rolls around. Some of the pieces of my dreams will fall into place. I will find myself at the bow of a skiff, Madaket Harbor will be glassy, some fish will reveal themselves, and I will start a cast: the realization of my winter's dreams. Rather than land softly in front of the cruising school, my deceiver will end up around my head, the line having been stepped on, been snagged, or mysteriously woven into an intricate bird's nest. While I untangle the mess, which will undoubtedly be made worse by rushing in an attempt to get the fly in front of the still cruising fish, I will probably make a commotion of some kind, and the fish will flee in terror. At this moment, my immediate thought will be, "John Gierach is full of shit." I will be pissed off at fishing's literary greats and it will cross my mind that I read too much. Perhaps Gierach, McGuane and the rest of them have filled my head with a bunch of nonsense about fly fishing being beautiful, artistic, and a path to inner happiness. If I had cast a spinning rod at the fish I would presently have one on the line; there is nothing beautiful or artistic about the deceiver in my hair or the bird's nest in my line and I am most certainly not happy.

The answer to too much thinking, fishing or otherwise, is often to turn on the television. In most cases, the television will ease your mind by putting you into an intellectual stupor or by gradually making you dumber, but in this rare instance television is home to some real value and sage guidance. The two greatest fishing shows of all time are the *Walker's Cay Chronicles* and the *Spanish Fly*. Flip Pallot of the *Walker's Cay Chronicles* and the late great Jose Wejebe of the *Spanish Fly* are two guys who seem, at least through the magic of television, to have achieved balance in their fishing. Fly rods are usually present; they seem to be favored by Pallot and Wejebe if the conditions and the fishing circumstances are favorable, but neither hesitates to fish differently, and certainly, there is no joy lost when the fish are caught on lures, or trolling, or bait. It may be due to saltwater. Both shows were, if not exclusively saltwater, certainly saltwater dominated, whereas the aforementioned literary giants find most of their inspiration in the trouts.

My own trout fishing has been extremely limited, but in my experience, there better be something artistic and beautiful about getting the fish to bite, because if you are accustomed to saltwater fish, nothing that happens after they bite is going to be noteworthy. That is not really a fair thing to say, because in my life I have caught four trout (all on fly) and the largest went a little over a foot. And certainly that one footer shot around pretty good. But it is tough for a saltwater guy to get past the fact that occasionally, when setting the hook in a manner you perceive as gingerly, the fish is yanked out of the river and propelled into the air, bouncing off your chest and landing at your waist ready to be unhooked. To judge all trout fishing based on my limited experience would be like judging saltwater fishing after two trips on a Fort Lauderdale head boat, and that is ridiculous. I am not done with trout fishing, by any means, and I look forward to doing more of it. But even with my extremely limited experience, I do not think it would be unfair to say that much of its essence leads up to the bite, whereas in the salt, much of it occurs after. That is not to say trout are not admirable fighters, nor that presentation is negligible in saltwater, but merely that the focus shifts to some degree from one to the other, and therefore, the method of presentation matters more in regard to trout fishing.

Of course, fly fishing in itself is a reward in a way unlike any other type of fishing. When you are learning to fly fish, it is likely that many of your first casts were in your lawn, or in a field, or over a casting pool, whereas when you learned to cast a spinning rod, you were taken straight to a pond, beach or boat. While it certainly takes a degree of skill to cast a spinning rod, and to get a lure to land where you want it to, it is an accomplishment of a more utilitarian nature than being able to move a fly. I recently spoke with my buddy Toph, and he said he was finishing up a carpentry project mandated by his wife, and as a reward, was taking himself to his snow-covered lawn for some fly casting. It was practice, of course, but just moving the line in graceful loops without even the possibility of a fish, would be enough to make it a reward. If the main purpose of your fishing trip is just to leave the house, to get out there, unwind, lose yourself or find yourself, then that type of thing may be accomplished just by casting your fly rod, and you may go home successful despite having caught nothing. The pitfall there is the nagging possibility that you may have actually caught a fish if you had used a spinning rod.

In contemplating what makes me pick up a spinning rod over a fly rod or vis versa, I realize the ugly little possibility that vanity is a big factor in the decision. What makes me fish with a spinning rod until I catch one and then pick up a fly rod? I believe the idea of having caught "enough" is accurate, but who's "enough" is it? When somebody asks if I caught any, I want to be able to say yes, but why should I give a damn? When I got to Straight Wharf, I wanted to catch a lot of big striped bass to be in the same league with Josh and Bobby. I want to catch a permit on fly to have reached saltwater fly fishing's highest pinnacle when throwing live crabs at them would be about a hundred times more likely to end successfully. Does this mean I am fishing toward somebody else's idea of enough?

I was talking recently with my Uncle Bob about a fishing trip that will in all likelihood never happen. We were talking about where we might go for some good flats fishing given a short window, taking into consideration we would be traveling from Nantucket so we would have to add about a half day on both ends just to make it to a major airport. He suggested Key West for permit, claiming we would get into permit if we had two days of fishing. After a little more discussion, I said that the trip was going to go from theoretical to highly likely very fast if he thought we would both get fly rod permit in Key West in two days of fishing. He said he absolutely did not think that; he thought we were talking about fishing live crabs.

Uncle Bob is a fisherman virtually free of vanity. He fished through his youth as I did, but when fly fishing exploded on the Northeast saltwater scene he was in the prime of his fishing bum years and it affected him at least as much as it affected me. For years he was far more likely to be found casting a fly rod, but instead of forming him into a purist or causing him to view one type of tackle or method as superior, fly fishing was merely the vehicle that made him into a passionate angler. His angling is not subject to the latest trends or confines. He went through a fairly lengthy stage when fishing dead bait on the bottom with a funky old baitcasting setup was his preferred method, and I believe he still enjoys it. Among other things, he was intrigued by the variety of species that will eat a piece of bait off the bottom. On many trips to Florida or the Bahamas, through accident and circumstance at first, but now probably more by design, he has found himself bottom fishing while anchored on a patch reef. Upon his return home, it is these multi-species, action filled, low-pressure days that he talks about, telling me what a great time it was. Currently occupying the top spot of his list of species he desires to catch is the tautog.

It may be freedom from vanity and a total indifference to what happens to be en vogue amongst the hip fishing crowd that would lead my uncle to suggest I spend a vacation throwing live crabs. He suggested it would appropriately challenging, the permit being a difficult species, but there would likely be some success. He stated that he would rather permit fish with live crabs than fly fish for bonefish. He seemed lukewarm on a trip whose success depended on long odds, like a fly rod permit. His idea of a vacation was not about climbing angling peaks or the artistry of fly fishing; it was about fun, and there is certainly something to be said for that.

However, during the same conversation without any prompting from me, he spoke about the idea of enough. He declared, more or less, that he had caught "enough" bonefish, and the permit was the one with allure now. And at least for the time being, the most pressing concerns in regard to his permit fishing are numbers and size rather than method. He has already caught one permit on fly, which I suppose is enough, at least temporarily; the literature suggests that nobody will ever catch enough permit on fly.

If Uncle Bob, an angler happy and content to go through a squid on the bottom phase in the midst of an angling career with a resume that includes a familiarity and competence with trout, bonefishing all over the Bahamas and elsewhere, and a permit on fly, is still influenced by the idea of having caught enough fish, then perhaps vanity is the wrong descriptor in what drives me, or what drives anglers. It is not so much that Bob and I are driven by different motivations, it is that we are in different places right now, and perhaps forever, in our pursuit of *enough*. Currently, I have not caught enough blue marlin (none), permit on fly (none), or enough bonefish on fly (several, but always one here, one there, and I am looking for a couple big days). Bob has not caught enough tautog (none), hogfish (I don't know where his hogfish tally currently stands), or enough and big enough permit.

The idea of enough is a difficult one for an angler to wrap his head around anyway. The existence of the angler's enough is called into question easily with *reductio ad absurdum*. Imagine a trip with a fishing pal, let's say he is on the bow of Rich Smith's skiff in "The Stadium", the tarpon Mecca between Marathon and Key West, and he makes a beautiful cast to daisy chaining tarpon. A big fish sucks down the fly. After a forty-minute fight including impressive aerials, a display of blazing speed across the flats, and a savage tug of war, the fish is brought alongside, photographed, released, and after the weary high-fives and a moment to catch his breath, your buddy says, "Well, that is enough for me. I suppose I will take up golf. Do you guys know anybody who wants some used fly tackle?" It is absurd to the core. No angler is fishing toward some predetermined goal with the idea of retirement after he reaches it. Pushing the idea of enough to its limit can take you to many different endings, each as absurd as the last: the angler so good he now fishes without hooks, the fisherman that now just walks to the river and looks at it rather than wet a line, etc.

Enough is funny; it is moving target, and in the end, it may not exist at all. I believe it is out there though, because sometimes, rarely, when everything comes together and the fish cooperate, you can sit and watch the sunset with enough sitting next to you. But the next day, you will wake to find enough has slipped away, leaving no trace except a happy memory, and there will be little to do other than chase it again. It is not important whether you chase enough with a spinning rod, a fly rod, or you troll around after it, what is important is that you chase it at all.

10

Tattoos

Chick is big into tattoos these days. I think they are very popular at his daycare and he and most of his buddies arrive sporting new tattoos all the time. A dinosaur on the forearm, a shark on the leg, or a racecar on the back of the hand are all tattoos you are likely to encounter at the reading circle and on the playground. Of course, these are the novelty tattoos, though the tattoos on the parents of Chick and his pals are the real deal.

Tattoos are nothing special in my generation. We are a fairly heavily inked bunch. I am not just talking about bikers and Navy men, but businessmen, doctors, lawyers, teachers, and people in all walks of life. Beneath their Brooks Brothers suits or business casual slacks you are likely to find a few tattoos. I am all for it. I have two myself. I am currently considering one or two more in the near future, and I would not be opposed to ending up with a dozen or more.

Chick's familiarity with tattoos enables him to recognize mine. Occasionally he will point to my right leg above my ankle and say, "Dada, you have tattoo?" and I will say yes. The other day, he was running around my bedroom when I was changing my shirt, and he said, "Dada, you have a fish tattoo on your shoulder?" and I said yes. He replied it was time for a new shark tattoo on his arm, and off he went with his mother to get some new ink by way of a wet paper towel. He does not yet understand the fundamental difference of our respective tattoos, but that day is in our future. And when that day arrives, tattoos will need to be discussed, and possibly even added to the disturbingly long list of discussion topics in which the clear theme will be do as say and not as I did. But I know that any blanket prohibition or firm stand against tattoos will be hypocritical and transparent, and therefore probably not carry much weight, and at this point I am not ready to wholly discourage or prohibit tattoos anyway. Instead, I will offer some lessons and thoughts, which will no doubt change in the coming years, but better to get something on the record now. Tattoo advice from a thirty-something dad who is actively considering more tattoos may be more valuable than both the overeager teen and the prohibitive Dad in his forties or fifties.

I cannot overlook the fact that my own predilection for tattoos did not spring from my generation's fondness for them, but rather from my own experience as a boy. My grandfather was tattooed, his coming from his time in the Navy during World War II rather than his time in college during the 90's or 2000's. They were blurry and monochrome, and they stretched down his forearms. I remember thinking that they were awesome and I decided that I too would get tattoos at some point. I remember declaring my intentions to be tattooed to my mother at a young age, and she paid me little mind. Probably because it was many, many years until I would actually be able to get a tattoo, and at that time in the eighties, tattoos hadn't yet become popular across the board and it probably was not something she was concerned about.

My intentions never wavered and when I went off to college, unlike my freshmen peers who began considering tattoos now that they were away from home and tattoos were popular and available, my mind was already firmly made up in favor of them.

My first piece of tattoo advice is to consider all possible tattoos for a minimum of one year from the point at which they become a possibility. It was legal for me to get a tattoo on my eighteenth birthday, but by imposing a one-year contemplation period I saved myself from a potentially ridiculous tattoo and instead got a beautiful tattoo that I am eminently pleased with and about which even my mother had nothing bad to say.

At first, and I have no idea where this idea came from, I wanted a cartoonish sun standing on Nantucket, smiling and waving. I was even considering a text bubble of some kind, though I thankfully forget what it was and I have no permanent reminder. After careful consideration for a year, I settled on an outline of Nantucket with a more realistic rendering of the sun setting over Nantucket Sound. I have always been pleased with the outcome.

The tattoo itself and the circumstances in which I got it have become one of the noteworthy milestones in my relationship with my mother, in which supremely irritating one another is the ultimate expression of love. She phoned me at college, days before my nineteenth birthday, to let me know that she hadn't gotten me anything and to pick something out and put it on the emergency credit card. I went to the tattoo parlor, had the tattoo done, and happily put it on the Visa. My mother called to wish me a happy birthday and to inquire as to what she got me, and I told her she had gotten me a very nice tattoo. Needless to say, it was not her ideal gift. I was going to get the tattoo anyway, with or without the birthday spending allowance, but I thought it nicely ironic that my mother would be paying for my first tattoo.

A few weeks later when I was home for Thanksgiving I showed it to her and she said, "Well, if you are going to have a tattoo, I guess that is a good one to have," which in the world of mothers commenting on son's tattoos, I believe is about as good as it gets.

My second tattoo is a blue marlin jumping out of the water in a tropical setting with some palm trees and the sun behind it. I never had second thoughts about my first tattoo, but if I had a do-over with this one, I may consider it. It is not because I do not like the tattoo, I love it. I would only consider changing the species, and I would only consider changing that because I feel like I may have jinxed myself by getting a blue marlin prematurely.

When I got the tattoo, it was meant as a sign of things to come rather than things already accomplished. I was still in college, a year and a half after my first tattoo, and though I didn't really have much of an idea as to what the future would hold, I knew that it should be centered on fishing. With real life concerns, such as a career and general adulthood looming, increasing conversations with friends about grad school, shitty jobs in finance, public relations, whatever the hell that is, and shared apartments, I felt it was important to get a permanent reminder of true priorities. I decided to emblazon my shoulder with a jumping blue marlin, a shining sun, and swaying palms. At that point, in terms of personal preference, my scale was tipped slightly toward the big game side rather than the fly fishing and flats side, and then, as now, billfish were held in high esteem. I had contemplated the tattoo for quite some time, at least my prescribed year, and I was very comfortable with the concept. It turns out I needed no reminders, help, or inspiration to keep fishing my priority, but it didn't hurt.

The only thing I was unsure of was the species of billfish. I seriously considered sailfish, white marlin, and swordfish, as well as the eventual blue marlin that won out. At the time, my experience with any billfish was purely imaginary, literary or through television. As far as real billfishing went, I had been skunked more than a couple times on sailfish charters. I considered the sailfish because at the time it seemed like the most accessible billfish, and would probably be the one I would first get some experience with. In fact, if I had caught a sailfish on one of my charters, I probably would have gone with one in the tattoo, but I figured since I was getting a tattoo of a fish I had never caught, it might as well be of a big fish I had never caught. I considered the swordfish because of its presence in my home waters and its exalted status. However, at the time I was considering the tattoo, South Florida's rejuvenated swordfishing was just getting good and getting noticed, and I was largely unaware of it. I felt there was a decent chance I would never catch a swordfish in my whole life, and while I was comfortable getting a fish I hadn't caught yet, I wanted it someday to become I fish I had caught. I deemed the sailfish too small, and the swordfish too rare, and the white marlin both small and rare (Nantucket then being a few years into our decade-plus white marlin drought), and the blue marlin became the winner.

Now, a little more than a decade after the tattoo, pretty much all my thinking was way off base. I have caught many sailfish in South Florida and Costa Rica, as both a captain and an angler, I caught a swordfish one night under a full moon in the Gulfstream off Miami, and have caught a couple white marlin about twenty miles south of Nantucket. A blue marlin has still eluded me. Looking back, I cannot recall what scenarios I thought would play out in which I would catch a lot of blue marlin. Perhaps I thought I would be the captain of a private sportfisher traveling to all the marlin hotspots, a career I did desire and pursue for a time, but never really got close to, or perhaps I thought my law career would be extremely lucrative and I would find myself with a budget that permits fishing for blue marlin often, or perhaps I had visions of taking my charter operation south and offshore. Whatever I was thinking, it sure didn't turn out, and the blue marlin tattooed on my shoulder is the only one I have come in contact with.

I have had a few run-ins. While running the charter boat out of Miami during my last year of law school, we were trolling for dolphin one day in the spring. I found a large palm tree floating and we were getting pretty consistent dolphin bites. After a number of productive passes, followed by probably three unproductive passes, I was considering moving on when we got a violent strike. I heard it before I saw it; the outrigger bent dramatically before the line popped out, and shuddered violently back and forth for quite some time afterward. There was nothing but a crater of white water where the lure was running a moment ago, and line was melting very quickly off the Penn International from which we were running the largest lure in the spread. My mate, named Lee, was a good fisherman and a nice guy, and he had some blue marlin experience. He said he saw the take, and thought it was a marlin.

The excitement was short lived. Very unceremoniously, the line just stopped leaving the reel and we had a slack line. I quickly moved the boat forward and somebody, I don't recall if it was Lee or our customer, cranked furiously in hopes the fish had just turned and still had our hook in its mouth, but it was no use. The hook had pulled. Upon retrieving our leader, Lee felt the leader, which was lightly chaffed a couple feet up from the lure, the work, he said, of a marlin's bill. Perhaps Lee was being optimistic (or is it pessimistic when you lose the fish?), but a blue marlin seems as likely a suspect as any other fish I can think of, and certainly, in the vicinity of a floating palm tree packed with dolphin is an excellent place to find a blue marlin.

My next encounter was when I was running a boat in Costa Rica and we were trolling a typical Central American spread of two large, hookless teasers close, and three ballyhoo on circle hooks farther back. My mate at the time was a fellow named Kevin. He was an amiable fellow with a lot of knowledge on engines. He was fairly new to fishing, but given my reciprocal lack of knowledge when it came to the engine, I was more than happy to have him along in the unfamiliar waters. He had become an expatriate because he had amassed several drunk-driving charges in the United States, and was reasonably sure that upon his next drunk-driving offense, he would find himself behind bars for not a short period of time. Faced with the prospect of giving up drunken driving or giving up his country, he chose his country, and moved to Costa Rica where he felt he could continue driving drunk without consequences. His plan worked for the time that I knew him there, but the thing that people prone to drunk driving do not seem to grasp is that drunk driving successfully without incident for a time does not rule out a tragedy the *next* time.

In any case, we were out fishing on a charter one day and a blue crashed the teaser. Until that moment, the Costa Rica sails had come to the teasers as I had been told to expect them, batting at it with their bill, and puffing their sail, and generally making themselves known and working themselves into a frenzy, and we had smoothly and successfully completed a few bait-and-switches, getting the sailfish to eat a ballyhoo dropped back on a circle hook while the teaser was removed.

The blue, however, had no intention of playing with the teaser; its intention was to eat it. I saw it charge into the spread, but before I could even yell "fish" it had the entire teaser in its mouth. I pulled on the teaser line, and the marlin and I had a pretty good tug-of-war for a while. Kevin started to pitch it a ballyhoo on one of our sailfish rods, but I recommended in an excitable tone that he pitch it the marlin bait we had on a 50-wide setup instead. After a little while, the marlin let go of the teaser and I pulled it out of the water. Kevin had the big bait in the water, but the marlin had drifted out of sight. I threw the teaser back in the water and hoped, but the marlin never reappeared.

When I went back to Costa Rica for my previously mentioned fishing bachelor party, we raised a blue marlin on our last day. John Brennan yelled down, and I picked up the 50-wide setup with a big mullet rigged with a circle hook. The marlin danced back and forth under the teaser. I could only catch glimpses, but John yelled down from the tower that it was a big blue marlin.

I quickly had the big mullet out behind the teaser and our mate quickly had the teaser coming toward the boat. The fish came up and his bill came out behind the mullet. My thumb was on the spool ready to drop the mullet back. The marlin gave the mullet a tentative tap with his bill, and then glided down into the depths while John yelled, "No! No! No!" from the tower, pleading with the fish to make a reappearance.

To claim that I am cursed or jinxed after these three brief encounters may be premature. They are difficult to find, hard to hook, and very hard to keep on a hook, so expecting to catch one in only three encounters may be asking a lot. On a recent episode of the *Spanish Fly* I learned that Jose Wejebe encountered twenty-seven blue marlin before landing one. On the other hand, it is certainly not *good* luck when a teased and hot marlin gives your mullet just a slight tap before changing its mind and heading back to the depths.

Perhaps a billfish tattoo of any kind at that point in my life was premature, but like I said, it was more of a reminder of priorities and a statement of aspiration rather than a declaration of knowledge or experience. And that remains true, the dream and aspiration of the blue marlin is still on my mind, and forever on my left shoulder. However, if questioned about my tattoo, I would much prefer to say that, "Yes, I have caught a blue marlin," or even better "I have caught several blue marlin," rather than offer an explanation about dreams and aspirations, especially since I am a professional fishing captain. It would be one thing if I were an accountant with unfulfilled dreams and aspirations of marlin. It is quite another to be a sportfishing captain. My growing billfish experience does mitigate this to some degree. For instance, now if asked about the tattoo, I can simply reply that it is a marlin, and yes, I have caught a marlin.

In fact, the tattoo could easily be a white marlin. Its dorsal is maybe a hair too pointy and it is a tad too bulky in the shoulders, but nobody would know that except me. And I suppose that is the point: I am not as comfortable with a tattoo built on dreams as I would be with a tattoo built on experience. Instead of becoming comfortable with it, I would rather just catch a blue marlin.

Mike remains untattooed. Once, when we were shark fishing with Bill Palmer, waiting and watching our balloons, and in need of a discussion topic, I recommended he get a black sea bass tattooed across his face and cheek with its mouth open as if it were about to eat Mike's eyeball. When he objected to getting the tattoo of his own accord, we discussed how much somebody would have to pay him to get such a tattoo. He seemed to think that such a tattoo would ensure he never made a new friend and remained single for life, so the price was quite high. Eventually the conversation turned to tattoos Mike may actually consider. Mike is a known lover of trout, and I, being somewhat ignorant of trout hierarchy, suggested he get a tattoo of a rainbow trout. He became indignant and told me he would never consider a rainbow trout tattoo. If he were to get a trout tattoo it would be of the wily and beautiful brown. For some reason, it was presupposed the tattoo would be on his rear end, probably because I insisted that is where it would be because that is the funniest place for a fictional tattoo. This led to many hours and weeks of juvenile yet entertaining joking about the brown trout in Mike's pants. The funniest were imitated dialogues of Mike meeting girls in bars and the ensuing conversation about the tattoo. For years now, when fishing or conversation lags, I can get a laugh by reciting "Hello, I'm Mike and there is a brown trout in my underpants."

I have considered my next tattoo for more than a year, but I have still not gotten it. For my second anniversary, I was planning on having a portrait of my wife, though with the tail of a mermaid, inked on my right shoulder. I find this nicely imaginative, appropriately nautical, and romantic as hell. I have not gotten it yet because my wife found out about my intentions and tried to talk me out of it.

My wife is a seemingly incurable snoop. If my email is accidentally left open on the computer, or she clicks on gmail and my inbox just pops up, she will scour the correspondence for as long as time will allow. If she somehow gets a hold of my password, she will actively check my mail. Nothing good has ever come of it. I have no idea what she is looking for. I do not think she suspects me of marital infidelity. I do not get to fish nearly as much as I would like with one woman in my life; having a girlfriend to further limit my fishing time while trying to keep two women happy and secret from each other sounds to me like a special section of Hell.

Sometimes she tries to defend her actions by saying you don't keep secrets from your wife. That may be true for the most part, but you also don't need your wife to spoil her gifts, and you certainly don't need to discuss the possibility of every potential fishing trip. From November to April a week seldom passes that I do not email somebody and suggest that we go fishing somewhere. My outbox is packed with emails that say things like "What are your thoughts on heading down to Costa Rica for an extended weekend to fish with John Brennan," or "Why don't we try and get to the Keys for a weekend to fish with Rich Smith," or "It's been a while since we fished with Matt Mitchell in Pine Island, how are your spring weekends looking?" Most of the people I email have their priorities all out of whack, and it is rare they even entertain the idea. A tiny percentage of the trips I suggest actually come together. Nonetheless, when Liz finds an email to a fishing buddy that suggests five days in Costa Rica, I will promptly hear yelling: "You are NOT going to Costa Rica. Who said you could go to Costa Rica? I can't believe you are planning a trip to Costa Rica!" or something to that effect. Then we will need to have a long talk, one in which she is probably starting out unhappy, about going to Costa Rica. Of course, I will be hesitant to say, "Honey, don't worry I'm not going to Costa Rica," because there is always a chance, however slim, that the email recipient will get back to me and say they are available and it sounds good. If that is the case, I want to make sure I am not committed elsewhere so I am left with the much less convincing, "Honey, don't worry, there is only a tiny chance I am going to Costa Rica."

I wouldn't plan a trip anywhere without her approval, but I also do not see the point in troubling her with the possibility of all the trips. The appropriate time to let her know about it is if I get some tentative yeses and possible dates in response to the email, at which time she will be brought into the loop and I will attempt to gain permission and her blessing.

It is this snooping that has caused a delay in my tattoo. She read my email to the tattoo parlor with my request, and then asked me not to get it. If you are going to get a tattoo in the likeness of somebody else, it seems like quite a setback to have her come out against it. However, I have given this some thought, and as with all tattoo matters I have contemplated it for months rather than hours. I think modesty demands she come out against it, and therefore I am going to ignore her. For instance, if the shoe was on the other foot, and she was considering a tattoo of me, it would be bizarre and in bad taste if I immediately came out strongly in favor of it. "Yes honey, I definitely think you should get my face tattooed on your back. Do you need me to pose for the tattoo artist?" is not something I, nor anybody else, should be comfortable saying. However, just showing up with a tattoo of the one you love is undeniably romantic.

She has also come out as being against more tattoos in general, but when it comes time to advise our children on tattoos, she will also be speaking from experience. On her ankle, she has a small Jesus fish and she does not really like to discuss it. A Jesus fish was an interesting choice, given that she is Catholic and to my knowledge the fish symbol is more often associated with other brands of Christianity. But a symbol of Christ is a symbol of Christ, and there is no need for any argument about a fish or a cross or whatever. Her Catholicism is also either historical or theoretical because since I have known her she has been to Church as many times as I have, which is twice: once for our wedding and once for our son's baptism. However, she was the one who wanted the wedding to be in a church and insisted the baptism take place, so I suppose her Catholicism isn't completely dormant.

She has occasionally expressed mild regret about the tattoo, and I have suggested it would be an easy fix. The Jesus fish and the Atlantic bonito have a very similar shape. A tattoo artist could add in some fins, some stripes, and some green, and in no time she would have a tattoo on her ankle of *Sarda sarda*, one of my favorite, and more importantly, one of her favorite species. For some reason this suggestion has not gained any traction yet.

After considering the mermaid tattoo for more than a year, and considering my wife's objection for almost a year, I am very close to pulling the trigger on it. My wife and I were at a fundraiser a couple weeks ago, and there was a gift certificate for a tattoo being raffled off, and she suggested I enter. I am going to take this as a passive gesture of approval and go for it.

It has been more than a decade since my last tattoo and it is time to get moving. Though my next piece of advice is that with tattoos, it is important to remember that you only get one canvas. There is a limited amount of usable space. A few acquaintances of mine were fast out of the gate and by their early twenties they had two full sleeves. I objected in theory, not because I frowned upon tattoos, or even bold tattoos, but because if they decided at a later date that wanted more tattoos, they may not have room for them. If they met a beautiful blond, married her, and desired some kind of over the top romantic gesture, they would not have any room on their shoulder for her likeness as a mermaid. If I decide at age forty, fifty or sixty, that I want another tattoo, I would like a place to put it.

Additionally, while you are young, you probably should not get any tattoos that are not covered by pants and sleeves. There may be times in your life when you want your tattoos concealed. Meeting your significant other's parents and job interviews come to mind. This may be less of an issue these days, since there is a good chance the thirty or forty year-old person interviewing the twenty-something has a few tattoos himself, but nevertheless, a tattoo on the leg or shoulder says one thing, and a tattoo on your neck says another. For better or worse, visible tattoos may close some doors, and through your teens and twenties, keeping doors open should be a prime consideration. On the other hand, what is the point of getting a beautiful piece of body art if it is going to be permanently hidden from the world?

Additionally, on my tattoo horizon, I have been considering a band of fish swimming around a limb for years. I even doodled it from time to time, but nothing concrete ever took shape, perhaps because of my limitations as an artist, and it has remained only a thought and a possibility since college. Currently, my favorite television show is *Californication*, and the episode when Charlie Runkle gets a butterfly tattooed on the small of his back is really fantastic. In the same episode, David Duchovny's character, Hank Moody, gets an anchor tattooed on his shoulder blade. Wrapped around the anchor are banners with the names of his daughter and the love of his life. I was considering duplicating it with Liz and Chick on the banners. However, if my inspiration for that tattoo is discovered, it will require yet another talk with Chick, this one about the content of

137

Californication. I am also considering some kind of symbol of learning, books, or knowledge. I would appreciate the irony of a tattoo celebrating that sort of thing, rather than the more traditional skulls, snakes, devils, and generally tough stuff. I think this would be especially effective in the classroom. If students asked about tattoos, I would get a kick out of showing them one celebrating homework.

But for now, contemplate is what I will do, and perhaps if I ever actually get Liz as a mermaid on my arm, I will start the clock ticking on my year of contemplation for the next one.

11

In Pursuit of Marital Balance

"I fish all the time when I'm at home, so when I get a chance to go on vacation, I make sure to get in plenty of fishing"
- Thomas McGuane, *The Longest Silence.*

I am sitting in a cozy room, with a fireplace and jacuzzi, in the Haraseeket Inn, in Freeport, Maine. It is exactly the kind of place, that as a single man, you would not stay. In fact, you wouldn't even consider staying here, and it is difficult to picture a time in your future when you would stay in a place like this. Now, married, I am here. And it is not even my first time.

When we were dating, I got Liz a trip here for Christmas because it was all she wanted, and what else is a man to do? I figured, go once, get it over with, and you'll never have to do it again. If Liz likes bed & breakfasts that is fine, but in the future we will go to bed and breakfasts that are both warm and have accessible fish. Even after we left the first time, she essentially agreed that it was not something we needed to do regularly. Yet here we are, back again, and this time I had to spring for the jacuzzi and the fireplace, as opposed to just the fireplace which we had last time. Though, to be honest, that was as much my doing as hers, figuring that if we must go north to a bed and breakfast, we might as well do it in style.

Liz is here for the shopping, the atmosphere, the relaxation, and perhaps the quality time as a couple, and there are few places she would rather be. I am here in pursuit of marital balance and a big deposit in my fishing savings account. The list of places I would rather be is long, but in the interest of happiness, and future fishing trips, both on my own and as a couple, I am here.

My wife goes through most of her days feeling like she does at least seventy-five percent of the work necessary to keep our family functioning in society. These tasks include making money, paying bills and buying groceries with the money, cooking, cleaning, child-care, laundry, and in general anything that must or should be done, but not something we necessarily want to do. The paradox is that I too spend most days under the impression that I shoulder about seventy-five percent of the daily workload.

In thinking about why this is, I would guess that upon parenthood there is so much more work and responsibility than you could imagine while single or childless, that when faced with it, you naturally assume you are doing somebody else's work in addition to your own portion, and unfortunately, when it comes to identifying the loafer responsible for your increased workload, your spouse is the only logical suspect. Of course, this applies only to *most* cases. In my case, I really do shoulder about seventy-five percent of the work.

Occasionally, this results in disagreements but not nearly as many as you would think between two people spending most of their days under the impression that they are somehow carrying a portion of the other's load. Most of the time, I cheerfully shoulder my load, real or imagined, because in my mind it entitles me to do as much fishing as possible (both at home and involving travel). I am working hard not only at caring for my family, but I am socking away time in my fishing savings account.

My wife shoulders her load because she is generally cared for and she gets to make the vast majority of daily decisions. First, she is cared for as a diner. From approximately mid-October until May, she can essentially order her dinners as if in a restaurant, and she gets nearly total control of the family menu. Chicken piccata is her current favorite, and therefore we have chicken piccata as often as once a week, but at least twice a month. Past favorites included baked stuffed shrimp, chicken parmesan, and fajitas, and comparatively the prep and cooking time for chicken piccata isn't too bad, which puts me in no position to complain.

A few nights ago, she was in the mood for a chocolate desert, and I made her a chocolate ganache cake. It was a several hour project, during which I would have preferred to be hunting, reading, or engaged in some other activity of fun or leisure, or perhaps even working on a project of my own: tying flies, building something, or writing. But, Liz ordered a decadent chocolate dessert, so a decadent chocolate dessert it was, and to some degree it was done because of the vague and largely unspoken assumption that my efforts would result in a fishing trip at some point in the future. But looking at chocolate ganache cake solely as a vehicle to a future fishing trip is cynical and not the entire picture. First, my time in the kitchen is work, but for the most part, it is a labor of love. I enjoy cooking. Also, a chocolate ganache cake is its own reward. It is rare that my wife is in the mood for a decadent chocolate dessert, and all it took was an off-hand suggestion to start me baking, happy for the excuse to indulge myself. I sometimes need a little more convincing on chicken piccata, especially if the requests become too frequent.

To say that I cook for my wife purely out of household necessity would be wrong, necessity would result in chicken piccata from a bag or some other premade garbage, or perhaps no chicken piccata at all. A request for a decadent chocolate dessert would result only in a trip down the frozen food aisle at Stop & Shop for a box of the little frozen lava cakes. Time could be spent hunting and tying flies rather than at the stove. There is extra effort and extra care taken, in part because of a love of cooking, in part due to a love of quality food, but most importantly out of love, kindness, and trying to do something nice and special for somebody you love.

Liz would say that I am completely full of shit. She would claim to prefer some kind of pre-made, pre-packaged garbage to the meal I prepared from scratch and argue that the only reason that I went to the trouble is that I am an unrelenting food snob. Not only is preparing a delicious feast not considerate or magnanimous, it is selfish in the extreme because I have dirtied most of the pots and pans in the kitchen that now need to be cleaned. Over the course of our relationship, things have changed. My wife, to her honest surprise, is becoming something of a foodie herself. After a steady diet of home cooking, and my preference for making things from scratch, she may claim to prefer a packaged product without the mess, and perhaps even from time to time find some comfort by indulging in junk-food, but for the most part, her expectations of quality in her food have risen dramatically. She has discovered she has a remarkably sensitive palate, capable of detecting and savoring very subtle flavors that go undetected by me. In the alternative, if even a hint of a spice or herb that she is not fond of goes anywhere near one of her dishes, I am lambasted. While she once claimed that chicken fingers and ketchup were her favorite meal, she will now request braised short ribs for dinner and upon tasting the fruits of my labor, perhaps even comment that they are not my best effort.

For my part, I have honestly tried and improved dramatically at cleaning as I cook. A practice I am told good chefs embrace. I am most often told this by people with very spotty records in the kitchen and I never see Emeril or Bobby

Flay doing the dishes, but now that I am getting the hang of it a little bit, it does seem to make sense. It certainly cannot be overlooked that I love the food too, so perhaps the only thing that is purely altruistic is when my wife arrives to a delicious meal and the kitchen is already clean.

In addition to getting to choose the vast majority of our menu, she gets total control over the television. This does not bother me much at all. I would usually prefer to be doing any number of other things, except at times she declares that not only will she be watching some kind of god-awful nonsense on television, but she will require company while watching. I am even happy with this because the television and my fly-tying desk share a room in our basement. I can happily tie flies while my wife watches whatever it is she wants to watch, and we can engage in some conversation or just be together. However, at times, she requests (demands) that I be present in our bed while she watches some terrible thing, and this I don't understand. Not only does she want to watch something awful on television, she wants me to suffer through it as well. I am not sure if this is common in relationships and marriages or if this is a rare phenomenon that I am subjected to. I want my marriage to stay young, I want the romance to thrive, I want a love and a passion on my twentieth anniversary more intense than I could have imagined on our wedding day. But also there is hope that some day my wife will not need or want me by her side to watch "Cupcake Wars".

But for the time being, I sometimes take in an episode of "Cupcake Wars" or some other equally stupid and disturbing nonsense, complete with back-rubs and Ben & Jerry's deliveries during commercials. I complain, but I don't complain as much as anybody who is forced to watch "Cupcake Wars" is entitled to, because it is a deposit in my fishing saving account that I will withdraw at some point in the future.

The fishing savings account is probably something we all deal with in one way or another, even as single, unencumbered, fishing bums. As a single man I never needed to watch reality television, but there were some things other than fishing in life that need to be accomplished, thought it was much easier to keep that list manageable. For instance, a single man may need to take a sunny May Saturday morning and change the oil in his truck, wishing instead that he could go fishing, but that sunny May morning deposit will keep his truck running all summer, and keep getting him to the fish. Something is sacrificed with the idea that fishing will come later, the difference being that the interest rate in the fishing savings account for single dedicated angler is about one thousand percent, it drops significantly for the married man, and plummets to a rate you may get at a real savings account for the parent.

Here I sit in this very pleasant room in a very pleasant inn, for the promise of future time on the water. There are some very nice trout just down the street, but they are in an indoor trout pond at L.L. Bean, and you are not supposed to fish for them; at least I assume you are not supposed to fish for them, the sign just said not to throw coins. There are probably some wild trout, as in not indoors, close by and maybe even some real wild trout, as in not from a hatchery. There may also be some ice-fishing. But I am not here to look for trout, or any fish for that matter. I want to maximize my deposit, and looking for trout in January in Maine seems like a cold and foolish withdrawal.

This trip runs contrary to pretty much every idea I have about a good vacation, yet none of it is disappointing at all. I am of the school of thought that vacations should not be spent doing something you can do at home. An odd statement perhaps for the non-angler to comprehend, given I can and do fish often at home, but it makes perfect to the angler. For instance, I have never fished for stripers or bluefish on vacation.

If I am going to travel and spend a significant amount of money, why would I do it to catch a fish I can catch at home, or perhaps more accurately, when I live in one of the best places on earth to catch those species. If I am traveling, I would like to catch new and different fish: bonefish, permit, tarpon, billfish, redfish, snook, and the list goes on.

But the idea of doing something on vacation that I cannot do at home extends beyond fishing. For instance, my wife cites relaxation as a prime goal for vacations. Sleeping late and reading in front of the fireplace are priorities. My question is why the hell do we need to go to Maine in order to sleep late? Sleep as late as you want on Nantucket, then spend the day on the couch with a book. We do not have a fireplace, and I understand that is a draw, but it is really worth the drive to Maine?

On vacation, I want to be on the move. Squeeze every drop. Sleep on the plane home. There are probably many single people out there, and even some couples, adventurous types, thinking: Yes! that is my idea of vacation. Come home happy and exhausted, with plenty of pictures and full of stories, catch up on sleep the next week in your own bed. And every parent out is thinking: good luck, you poor, stupid bastard.

I understand the appeal of a vacation from your responsibilities. A day to sit around and read, or lounge in a bath, or take leisurely lunches at cafes, or all of the above sounds pleasant, but it is all possible on Nantucket. As a single man, I could do all of the above, and in fact I did, especially when I was living with my parents and they went away, which was a type of vacation in itself. They had a fireplace I could read in front of and a large tub with jets to lounge in, and I could eat out or cook at my leisure. One of my favorite activities was to buy and cook an obscenely large steak and eat it in front of the fireplace and the television while watching a movie.

With plenty of relaxation available when I wasn't on vacation, the thought of going somewhere to relax held little appeal. I may totally lose my mind if forced to take a typical "beach vacation" full of warmth and sun and lounge chairs. On one hand, a Caribbean beach would be nicer than heading north, since I am partial to warm rather than cold weather, but on the other hand, if I were forced to 'relax' at and around a beach resort all day it would grate on me all day that though I may not be at the right spot, I am least in the right climate for some excellent saltwater action. Having taken a long plane ride south to eventually relax would be to experience the pain of having your dream snatched away only moments before it was in your grasp.

But upon parenthood, the need for a vacation to relax skyrockets, and furthermore, the success of the vacation may depend on putting some real and tangible distance between you and home. Everybody, parent or not, probably understands this. You may be able to skirt your responsibilities and delay your obligations when you are home, but putting some miles between you and the responsibilities surely makes it easier. Bosses, parents, children, and spouses can all make it difficult to relax at home. That goes without saying, but sometimes the biggest culprit in robbing you of relaxation is yourself. Some people are capable of total relaxation even in the midst of obligation, whereas others will not be able to relax at all. Even in the absence of obligation they will create and invent tasks ad infinitum. I would place myself nicely in the middle of this scale, and my wife would place me closer to the side capable of relaxation through adversity, a trait she may cite as a flaw. On the other hand, she would place herself very close to incapable of relaxation, and I would favorably slide her a little more toward the middle, the capacity for relaxing in my view being worthy of praise. For all but the most chronic relaxers, for whom the miles are totally unnecessary, putting distance between you and your home will certainly help with relaxation. For instance, here at the Haraseeket, it is impossible for me to cook anything, clean my basement, or build, fix, or install any number of things around house. It is also highly improbable that my mother will visit to comment on my work ethic and perhaps invent a task or errand for me. While she is here with me, it is also highly improbable my wife will have a task for me other than perhaps make a dinner reservation, because she is the one that mandated this vacation of relaxation. As for Chick, physical separation from him is absolutely necessary for any elongated period of relaxation.

It took a little effort, but I have not had to try too hard in order to appreciate this fishless vacation. It also occurs to me, much like people needing to be away from home, for me it is important to be far away from fishing in order to get any real relaxation done. If there were any kind of angling opportunity around, I would be busy doing it, searching it out, or in the worst case scenario, having its existence weigh on my mind as I attempt to relax with Liz. I am having a very nice time in a very pleasant place and I think I am doing a pretty good job of making the best of it.

But make no mistake, I am making the best of it. Vacations, by their very nature, are limited. You need time and money, two things that just about everybody on earth wishes they had more of. I have been pretty lucky, I suppose, and most times I have only been short on one or the other, but being short on either still means adios to the vacation. The fact that both time and money evaporate much quicker with children in the picture makes vacations that much more precious. It is one thing to spend a day, or days even, doing some non-fishing around home. On Nantucket, it easy enough to say tomorrow is another day, but odds are that tomorrow is probably not another vacation day. No matter how vaguely pleasant and unobjectionable it may be to be relaxing here in Maine, it is irksome to spend a vacation without a rod in my hand.

In order to remain pleasant and gracious when that thought enters my head, I must remember that it is Liz, and not me, who has earned the right to complain. She has endured some tough times on vacation largely because of my unbridled desire to have a rod in my hand. In particular, a trip I took her on while we were dating comes to mind. In the planning stages, I asked repeatedly what her priorities were for vacation, and I was told she just wanted to relax in the sun, and if there was a beach with some chairs and hammock, she was going to be happy. I was after bonefish, and specifically do-it-yourself bonefishing. Both my budget and the fact that I was taking Liz ruled out the idea of spending every day, or even most days, on a skiff with a guide. After some research, and bad advice from my Uncle Bob given out of his unyielding love for the Bahamas, I chose a little hotel on Mangrove Cay, Andros, Bahamas. I was sold on location because of the bonefish and I was sold on the hotel by the allegedly expansive, wadeable, productive flats just outside the door of my room. It was a pretty easy sell to Liz because the place was a little hotel run by an American couple and it had a nice bed and breakfast feel to it, and an allegedly nice beach right outside the door.

The biggest culprit in ruining the vacation was the weather. We had originally planned to go in April, but plane tickets were expensive and something else came up, and we switched it to February. That turned out to be a colossal mistake. When making the change, I knew I was taking a little risk weather-wise, but I thought to myself, it is the Bahamas, how cold could it be? The answer, it turns out, is uncomfortably cold. One day the female owner had to go around Mangrove Cay rounding up blankets in anticipation of record lows in the forties. The forties is nothing new for New Englanders, until you imagine a hut on the beach, well-designed to be as cool as possible, without heat, and luggage-wise, this was unexpected. The end result of course being that Liz and I spent one of the coldest nights of our lives on vacation in the Bahamas. As you can already guess by now, neither Liz nor I will ever be staying there again, and I would guess that Liz will never be travelling to Mangrove Cay again. Obviously, the owners of the place cannot be blamed for the weather, but in addition to the poor weather, I never saw a bonefish on their flat that turned out to be none too expansive (who knows if the weather was the culprit with that as well), the beach turned out to be none too nice, and the "restaurant" at the hotel turned out to be the male owner, whose talents in the kitchen were dubious, turning out meals on his schedule and not yours. Mangrove Cay and the hotel are both isolated enough that dining elsewhere was not much of an option.

When a trip starts falling apart as this one did, and the do-it-yourself fishing turns out to be vastly worse than expected, as it did, you start to place even higher expectations on the days of guided fishing you have planned. For this trip, I definitely wanted to do one day, with a possibility of another day while keeping an eye toward a limited budget. The proprietor of the hotel arranged a guide for me for one day. I said that my schedule was totally flexible, and I wanted to make sure my day of guided fishing took place under optimal conditions, and they assured me that conditions and the weather looked good for the day in question. When it rains, it pours, and in this case, literally. There were intermittent deluges throughout my day of guided fishing. All of which Liz shivered through, once again cold in the Bahamas, but now wet too, and she complained minimally if at all, seemingly knowing that a lot was riding on the outcome of the trip. The guide seemed nice enough, but his ignorance of the weather was irritating, and in the end it cost him another payday. If he had taken Liz and me on a sunny day, the lack of bonefish in front of the hotel would have virtually guaranteed that I hire him again, but after suffering through a miserable soaking, Liz was in no mood to endure another day on the boat.

Despite everything, it wouldn't be too hard to convince me to go back. If I ever find myself considering a trip for which the purpose is to catch very big bonefish on flies, Mangrove Cay would need to be on the list. Between deluges on the guided trip, I threw some flies at some truly large bonefish. I am no expert as far as bonefish are concerned, and I am not confident in my ability to provide you with an accurate estimate of weight, but I would guess conservatively that I saw three to five fish over ten pounds, with one or two significantly over ten. Of course, the casts I made to them weren't good casts, hampered to some degree by the howling wind that went along with the rain, and the casts that were adequate were ignored. I ended up catching a couple small fish at the end of the day from a school of a few hundred that was cruising around. Liz was mad that I didn't let her reel one in. I said if you wanted to fly fish, you had to learn to cast, to practice, to spend long hours; it wasn't the type of thing were you just get handed a rod, and afterward I felt pretty shitty about it. After she had sat in the skiff in the rain all day, the least I could have done was hand her my rod once I hooked my second little bonefish.

Liz will never be considering another trip to Mangrove Cay, and certainly, that trip played a significant role in my finding myself at a bed and breakfast in Maine. A trip as disastrous as that one really gets her quite a bit of leverage in discussing further vacations. On the other hand, a snow-enveloped weekend at a bed and breakfast in a Mecca of retail will surely plant Liz in a flats skiff again at some point.

In pursuit of this marital balance, there are lowlights. Liz endured a very long, very wet day on a skiff and then shivered all night during a record low on a fly speck in the Bahamas. I have endured the Gap. Do I browse, halfheartedly looking for the one or two items in the entire store that may fit me? Do I tag along with Liz mentally calculating her tab and translating that into tackle and trips lost in favor of surplus pseudo-hip clothing of dubious quality? Do I wait outside and try to kill time? Regardless, it is no way to spend a moment of vacation. But nothing should be judged by the lowlights, or at least by the lowlights alone. Everything about the Gap sucks, but that is not the whole picture. Occasionally, in pursuit of balance, I have to stay in romantic places with a touch of luxury, relax with good books in front of fireplaces, and have wonderful dinner dates with my wife. For her part, Liz has to occasionally travel somewhere warm and sunny, experience the splendor and beauty of the flats from a front row seat, and catch some fish. For me, it is difficult to fathom being on the bow of a skiff and wishing you were somewhere else (other than on the bow of skiff someplace with either less wind, more fish, or both), but perhaps it is possible. Perhaps next time Liz finds herself fishing the flats with me in the Florida or Caribbean sun, she will be dreaming of a bed and breakfast with a fireplace somewhere. For my part, stuck in Maine with champagne problems and a happy wife who owes me some fishing time is not a bad place to be.

12

In Pursuit of Bonefish and Good Timing

A Vacation Diary

When all the pieces fall into place, when enough diapers have been changed, when enough dinners have been cooked, when enough money has been socked away, and when enough nights have been spent in cozy bed and breakfasts, and a window of opportunity presents itself, it is time to go fishing. Perhaps even a trip planned for no other purpose than to fish.

A few months ago, Mike and I began planning a fishing trip. He had come back to Nantucket at just about the same time as the stripers, and we floated around Polpis Harbor for an afternoon, and talked about a fishing trip in the upcoming fall or winter. It is dangerous business to talk about and think about future fishing trips while out fishing. Each individual trip should be savored, and anticipation or lust for a future trip should not be allowed to get in the way of that. Not to mention, in this new life of mine, planning more fishing when I am lucky enough to be fishing is counting my chickens before they hatch, and could even be construed as downright greedy. In this case, though, I reasoned it best to get a trip discussed, planned and booked in late April and early May, and then Mike and I could do our best to forget about it for a few months while we squeezed every drop of the angling opportunities available to us over the summer. Then, as soon as our season was done, instead of the melancholy of facing another long winter, we would have a glorious week in the tropics waiting for us.

Mike had just returned from several months of trout fishing in Argentina and Chile on what he describes as the trip of a lifetime. From the pictures I have seen, I do not disagree. It would not be my trip of a lifetime, given it was for trout rather than my preferred saltwater gamefish, though it certainly seemed great and I wouldn't blink at giving it a shot myself sometime.

He reasoned that it would be near impossible to top his trip as far as salmoniods go, so this winter it would be on to saltwater. The first trip he mentioned was a bizarre expedition to the Philippines for tarpon. When he mentioned it, I was unaware of tarpon in the Pacific, except for the few in Panama and Costa Rica that have travelled through the Panama Canal (*Megalops atlanticus*). Due diligence required I do some research because I was unwilling to point this out to Mike only to have him prove me wrong. Early in his mating career, Mike once told some customers onboard *Topspin* that yellowtail were a fairly common catch off Nantucket at certain times of the year, and I have been holding that doozey over his head for years. I do not want to risk giving him any ammunition with a similar gaff myself, like claiming there are no tarpon in the Pacific, unless I am sure. I am glad I did the research because there is an Indio-Pacific tarpon (*Megalops cyprinoides*), and for all I know they may be found in great numbers in the Philippines. Though the fish do apparently exist, the trip on its face did not appeal to me much. If I want to tarpon fish, I will go to Florida, where I know they are found in great numbers and with great size, and while the Keys may be less adventurous than the Philippines, they are not without their charm and a whole lot easier to get to.

The second trip Mike mentioned was a Central American expedition for bonefish, and I quickly locked him in on that and immediately invited myself along. Despite extremely limited lifetime success (including the Mangrove Cay disaster) or perhaps because of it, I find fly rod bonefish, and in particular, do-it-yourself fly rod bonefish, increasingly desirous. Normally, I would not be so forward in including myself in someone else's adventures, but I felt in this case I needed to immediately put to bed any notions Mike may have had about going on this one without me. Given my wife and child, it would be a pretty easy mistake for him to make, assuming that I would not be interested in spending the winter in Central America. I myself realized that any trip of the duration of which Mike was considering was out of the question, but I figured I could finagle two weeks and perhaps more if there were some mitigating factor. Those details could be hashed out later. I figured Mike would head down early, bum around, do some exploring and get a feel for the place. In optimistic daydreams I pictured him having the place wired by the time I arrived, and he would pick me up or arrange transportation for me at the airport and I would immediately be whisked to a flat with bonefish and permit coming in on the tide.

We discussed this trip vaguely for a couple weeks. I was in favor of staying put more or less, while Mike was dreaming of a whirlwind tour of many destinations and several countries. My thinking was that it is extremely difficult to find and catch fish in a new place, and starting fresh every few days would make it that much more difficult. Just finding accessible, wadeable flats can be a huge challenge. If we stayed put for a while, we may crack a few more of an area's secrets. Mike favored the traveling approach, wandering the region, figuring we would stumble onto decent fishing here or there, and trying to squeeze as many different places and experiences out of his winter abroad.

My choice, almost from the start, was Guanaja, in the Bay Islands of Honduras. I had read an article about it in *Fly*

Fishing in Saltwater, and it had stuck with me. Like everybody, when I read a decent article in a fishing magazine, I am immediately ready to book my ticket to whichever place happened to be featured. Anybody with even a passing interest in fishing is susceptible to this. My father once read an article about marlin fishing off the Gulf Coast of Florida, and he was immediately intrigued. He summonsed me excitedly to his den, showed the article to me, and asked what I thought. He spent the afternoon and evening looking into flights, hotels, and schedules examining the possibility of a marlin fishing trip to Pensacola.

My father does not particularly like to fish offshore. He has never taken a vacation for the purpose of fishing in his life. Sometimes on family vacations he even skipped the fishing trips and my mother would be charged with taking me and my brother fishing while he golfed or explored. But a good fishing story in print made him forget all this, made him forget that he had no desire to travel to Pensacola when he got up that morning, and forget that he did not have a burning desire to catch a marlin. Miraculously, he also forgot that he did not like to fish offshore. He talked about possible dates and plane tickets.

I was not willing to shoot down a fishing trip, especially a marlin fishing trip, but Pensacola seemed dubious. While he was considering a marlin fishing trip, I wondered how to get him focused on Panama or somewhere that made more sense. By the next day, the spell of the article had worn off and our Pensacola marlin adventure was never given any more thought.

The same thing usually happens to me, I put the magazine down for a little while and I come to the gradual or sudden realization that I am not going marlin fishing in Pensacola. I am not going to Charleston for redfish. I am not flying to San Diego to try and catch a mako on a fly rod, and I am not going to Islas Secas, Panama, to fish with Carter Andrews. If the fishing in the article is alright, the writing is decent, and the weather where you're at is cold, it makes you forget some important details, but eventually these come back into focus. For instance if I am going to travel to marlin fish, Pensacola is probably not my best option, if I am going redfishing, my father's home in Southwest Florida is probably a better bet than Charleston, despite the success of the article's author and his guide on a chilly winter day. Nantucket has plenty of makos, and if I want to bob around all day trailing a chum slick, a cross-county flight is not necessary, and Islas Secas with Carter Andrews seems about as cool as it gets, but a quick look at the rates online is all it takes to put that one on the distant, post-windfall, horizon. But for whatever reason some potential destinations are not forgotten, and my desire to make it to Guanaja hadn't faded even years later. It had a lot going for it: plenty of bonefish, good wading along hard coral flats, and the distinct possibility of a permit. What may have done it for me from the start was the do-it-yourself fishing, and eventually, that is what did it for Mike too. We were on vacation to fish, and fish hard, and nothing else really mattered. Of course, you can fish pretty hard and pretty well at any number of bonefish lodges around the Caribbean, but that comes with a hefty price tag we wanted to avoid. We understand the value of guided fishing, and we planned on hiring a guide for a portion of our trip regardless of location, but for the remaining time, we wanted to be able to grab our fly rods, walk some beaches and wade some flats, and get some shots at bonefish.

In fairly short order, we had booked our trip to Guanaja. Mike's several months and my two weeks got shrunk down to a week, but that is to be expected, and I am in no position to complain about seven day fishing trips. And then, quite successfully I think, it was largely forgotten about for the summer. If we were still considering a trip, there would have been the incessant conversations about destinations, times, accommodations, etc., but once it was booked, there was not much left to talk about. Of course, it was mentioned from time to time, but not to the detriment of enjoying and experiencing the fishing under our noses.

***

I am off on the Steamship, watching Coatue and Great Point melt away as I leave my beloved Nantucket in route to another island, Guanaja, thousands of miles toward the Equator. Though the cold is a good thing to escape from, I suppose it is not the cold that I escape from, but the fish that I run to. However, my brother was running his tugboat on Nantucket Sound yesterday and he saw fish jumping around, so perhaps my departure is premature. Temperatures for the last several weeks have been mild, though high winds as well as a myriad of other things have kept me off the water for several weeks. My last sporting adventure was a ride around the moors west of Hummock Pond with my friend and fellow captain Josh Eldridge, looking for some frail and confused pheasants that had recently been stocked. Neither of us was under the delusion that it was high sport, but Josh is a lover of upland bird hunting, and as he said on the phone the night before, "they put them there for people to shoot, so it might as well be us." We ended up seeing two, and getting one, which I hope made a fine dinner for Josh.

Leaving ahead of some straggling bluefish, or maybe bass, does not upset me too much. Certainly the pheasants are not much of a draw; a small handful are conceivably quick-witted enough to survive more than a few days in the wild, but most of the birds are slaughtered quickly by hawks and by hunters. As far as sporting is concerned, it would be very easy for me not to return until April, and it crosses my mind that the only bad part of this trip is that it is only a week, but that is a dinosaur of a thought, a holdover from the fishing bum days. The only real drawback of the trip is leaving Liz and Chick.

***

I am sitting at the bar at Graham's Place, approaching the halfway point of what, to this point, has been a very unsuccessful trip if it is to be measured by the amount of fish caught. Mike and I are deep into the fly box and running low on ideas. I am here waiting out a rain shower, but in no particular rush to get back to the vicious beating the fish are giving me.

I did manage to catch and release one small bone. I will not call it a "baby," but his size was not exactly impressive. If it were an eight or ten pound specimen, then the trip would already be successful on some level, but declaring victory after the release of a fish with a weight somewhere south of two pounds is difficult. Pictures were taken to commemorate the catch, but I will not be posting them, sharing them or framing them, because my hand dwarfs the little fella to the point of embarrassment. In addition to the petite bonefish, I caught have one baby barracuda, one blue runner, and two diminutive snapper-esque fish.

Hour by hour, expectations are being revised downward. As is probably the case with any fishing trip, especially a trip with no other agenda to a far-flung destination chosen explicitly for the availability fish, expectations ran high. I had visions of big days on bonefish, and I dared to dream of permit. I never really speculated in detail. I did not expect or hope for a ten fish day, but at times I thought that perhaps by day three, I would have had some reel-screaming runs, some pictures for the wall, and a general feeling that the trip was a success. It crossed my mind that by day three I would have released many bonefish, and portions of my day at least would be devoted to finding permit. Now, I am in the position of hoping for the few glorious hours (or dare I say days) that make the trip. A bonefish seen, cast to, hooked and released this afternoon or in the morning will not erase the beating the we have taken so far, but it will dominate the memory of the trip to this point and put the last three days in the category of "paying dues" rather than any number of other unfortunate classifications such as "consistently poor fishing" or "tremendous waste of time and money."

Our research indicated that the Caribbean side of Central America would be at the tail end of its rainy season. We could expect a few showers, but only intermittently. The bright side was that we could expect few other anglers and the fish probably would not have seen a fly in months. Upon arrival we were disappointed by nothing. There were vast and easily accessible flats virtually surrounding our accommodations here at Graham's and it has never been difficult to find a fish to cast to. Our timing seemed to be excellent, because we flew down and over Hurricane Sandy, leaving the Northeast before its arrival and getting to the Caribbean well after it had passed. But apparently, despite missing Sandy by a several hundred miles on both ends and Sandy not really coming close to Guanaja to begin with, the big storm disrupted the weather in the entire Caribbean basin. Winds all week have been extremely varied, both in terms of direction and speed. The fish it seems, are a little freaked out, and not strapping on the feed-bag.

We have fished a couple days with an excellent local guide, Cassidy Hoyle, and he has been apoplectic about lack of bites. Many times he has mentioned that he would kill for clients with our casting ability on most days, and if conditions were at all normal, we would be doing some serious business. Surely, this is at least partially just good business: if the client is frustrated by the bonefish, keep him happy by making him feel like Lefty Kreh. At the same time, his sentiments seem genuine and I think he is taking the beating at least as hard as Mike and me. The fish are still tantalizingly visible and abundant. I have had more shots at bonefish in the first half of this week than in my entire bonefishing career combined prior to arriving.

Sitting here, staring out at the flats being pounding by rain and whipped by wind, I am sadly reminded, that my last several attempts at bonefishing, or any fishing trip for that

160

matter, have not been what you could call successful either. I really feel like I am due for a big day, and right now, I would be prepared to call anything north of three fish a big day. Prior to this trip, my last bonefish experience was a day with guide Rich Smith for the large and notoriously difficult fish of Biscayne Bay. Liz and I had gone to Miami, a good destination for me to do some fishing and her to relax by a pool. Rich and I had a great day, sharing stories, and also advice about how to improve our respective guide businesses. I had four good shots that day, and I surprised and impressed myself by putting the fly exactly where I wanted on three of them, and even the fourth was passable. Those South Florida fish showed about as much appetite, or lack thereof, as the Honduran ones have to this point. Rich said the weather was just a hair too cold for the bonefish to really turn on.

That Miami trip also included a half-day sailfishing with the legendary Bouncer Smith. I was hoping to introduce Liz to billfish, but there was not much of a sailfish bite off Government Cut that day. We had a good time, Liz caught some type of large jack off the bottom, and my buddy Zach was fishing with us and he caught a large kingfish. Bouncer and his mate are as good as it gets in terms of spending time on the water with knowledgeable, friendly and fun people. Bouncer said they really needed a strong cold front to push through for the sailfishing to pick up, which really drove me nuts. Surely, I could understand adverse conditions for sailfish or bonefish, but apparently our trip to Miami coincided with a tiny weather window neither nice nor nasty, no good for either, and I flew home fishless except for some little thing that ate my bonefish fly on a practice cast.

A couple years ago my parents decided to take us on a vacation for Christmas. The vacation destination choice was full of the usual difficulties of travelling with my family. My father wanted to golf and did not want it to be too hot, my mother wanted to lie on the beach and Florida in December was not hot enough, my wife was pretty much with my mother but did not want to be anywhere too remote, and my brother and his wife had their own desires. I was characteristically inflexible about going anywhere without superb fishing. San Juan, Puerto Rico was suggested, and a little research indicated that tarpon fishing in the San Juan Lagoon was pretty good and pretty consistent and while December was not a good time for big ones, little ones were abundant year-round. With baby tarpon seemingly available for me, sun for my mother, infrastructure for my wife, and golf courses for my father, and my brother and sister-in-law also happy, we left for Puerto Rico the day after Christmas. The weather was just terrible. It rained every day and at times it was honestly cold. Even with our bodies used to the New England winter, there were times you didn't want to leave the room without a sweatshirt. Liz and I were particularly despondent, experiencing record cold on back-to-back Caribbean vacations.

On the first day there, I spent the morning tarpon fishing with a guide and we got totally blanked, failing to get a single bite. I had booked and paid for a half day but we spent significantly longer than that looking for a single fish.

The weather was blamed. Both the captain and his boss repeatedly assured me that usually it is a very consistent fishery. They were very sorry. I said not to worry, I know how it goes and sometimes the fish don't cooperate. I gave them my phone number at the hotel and my email and told them to call me when the fish turned on because I would very much like to go again. They assured me things would be back to normal soon, extreme cold fronts in Puerto Rico being very rare and very brief, and they would be in touch. The cold and rain persisted, the tarpon didn't start to bite, and I never heard from them about another trip.

And of course, prior to that there was the Mangrove Cay disaster.

However, hope springs eternal in the heart and mind of a fisherman. The rain seems to be stopping and the wind seems to be laying down, and I will abandon my stool and my cup of coffee for now, and hit the flats for the last hour of daylight, with the hope that the fish will be more easily duped in the low light, and the day can be marked a success.

***

I am back to my stool having freshly spooked one small group of bonefish, and having my Chico's honey shrimp ignored by a group of others on a cast that I truly don't believe could have been improved upon. There was a group of about five fish, and I detected them coming at me down a shin deep channel between a sea wall and the reef. I laid my fly out before they got into range, waited, and then started stripping. Hopes ran high as the body of fish moved toward my fly as I began to strip. My fly moved slowly ahead of the school, and then slightly quicker, and then it was in the school. I was waiting for resistance to reach my fingers. I was ready for one of my strips to be halted, but it never happened. They took no notice of the fly, or at least none that I could detect. They overtook my fly and continued swimming toward me, until I could just about whack them with the tip of fly rod. Then they took notice of me, and vamoosed with a flourish.

It was the last in a series of memorable failures. This morning, I placed a lightly weighted Simram in the path of a bonefish that was dawdling along, at least apparently looking for food. Much to my delight, another previously unseen bone appeared in the vicinity and I was encouraged that a little competition would spurn one of them into eating. A couple strips had the desired effect, and both charged the fly with enthusiasm, only to execute a double refusal upon reaching it. On Monday, Mike and I were delighted to find several big bones cruising a shallow flat a stone's throw from Graham's Bar and Restaurant. I had one turn and follow a Gotcha memorably, but

163

it turned away before eating. Yesterday, when out with Cassidy, we found a school of bonefish that seemed happy enough, and we proceeded to throw a Crazy Charlie, a Peterson's Spawning Shrimp, and a Kwan to them. Mike worked the right side of the school while I worked the left, while the bonefish milled around undisturbed and also not disturbing our flies.

Mike suffered the most heartbreaking incident of the week, when a nice fish actually ate his fly with a swirl (a small crab of which I do not know the name, but has since been refused by many other bonefish). Mike set the hook with only the briefest resistance before the fly came back at him without a fish attached.

In addition to these failures to catch a fish, there have been countless other less memorable ones. Mostly Mike or I have cast to more or less where we wanted near a bone or bones, only to have the fly completely ignored. We have waited, we have stripped slowly, we have stripped quickly, we have stripped slowly then quickly, we have stripped quickly then slowly, and we have changed flies and done it again. Sometimes it ends with the fish moving away of its own volition, and sometimes it ends by us making repeated casts closer and closer in desperate attempts to have the fly noticed, eventually having the fly land on its head and the fish depart in swirl and panic. We have successfully scared the daylights out of many bonefish, and that has become a running joke, good for a cynical laugh. Mike and I will rendezvous after time apart on the flats, and to the question of "did you catch anything," the standard and unfortunately true response has become, "no, but I scared the shit of a few of them."

All the above uncaught fish could at least in part be blamed on the fish, but there have been many more in which the fault lies squarely on my shoulders. I have made first casts to unknowing fish, and not the fly but the line has landed squarely on top of them. I have made plenty of casts too far away from fish to have any reasonable hope of them seeing the fly. I have had wind knots and tangles, lines caught on rocks and my boots, and the rest of the usual assortment of fly-fishing mishaps. Cassidy found one school of fish he assured us was actively looking for food, and virtually assured me a hook-up if I could lay my fly on the edge of the school. I put my first two attempts well short and on the third shot the fly right over them, sending all of them scattering when my line landed on their heads

***

We awoke this morning to weather that was far from perfect, the wind lingered from the North, observations that it had swung slightly to the East (apparently the desirable direction for the fish both to be on the reef in big numbers and to bite) or that is was about to swing to the East were prominent, but they were more statements of optimism and hope than any actual reporting on the weather conditions. However, the sky was fairly bright and the wind, while still from the North, was as light as it had been all week. A new day, a brand new hope for bonefish. We grabbed our rods, tippets, and fly boxes, slipped into our flats boots and hit the reef. We crossed the little wooden bridge to the reef and succeeded, for probably the tenth time of the week, in scaring the daylights out of the two seemingly resident small schools within a quick walk of the bridge.

As we made our way down the flat, we saw Cassidy motoring up to Graham's. We rightly assumed he was coming to pick us up and we turned around. Arrangements had been made to fish another day, but they were made in a very fluid Central American way, dependent on a good weather and no concrete answer as to when that day would occur. Apparently it was today. We walked back to meet Cassidy and get some breakfast.

We ate and departed, heading North from Graham's toward flats adjacent to a little island where we had found promising sized schools of bonefish two days earlier. As usual, finding fish was not the problem, and after a ride of no longer than five minutes, Mike was at the bow and casting to some fish.

I was in the middle of the boat, also fishing. The school was moving around in water around four or five feet deep and with the school in a little deeper water, it made sense for us both to be fishing, laying our flies in the path of the school, letting our fly sink while waiting for the fish to glide over them, and then stripping.

Mike laid his fly in front of them, and began to strip as they overtook his fly, and then, his line came tight, his rod doubled and line flew from the deck. A hook-up! I reeled in my line, put down my rod, and started to unpack Mike's fancy camera from the dry bag.

"You are a lucky man with jacks," Cassidy said. Mike's fish was bulldogging him around under the boat, instead of burning off across the flat, and it was clear that for the second time this week an aggressive jack had literally emerged from amidst a school of bonefish to happily inhale Mike's fly. He landed the jack and I took a couple photos, and he was back at it. After another two accurate casts into the school that were ignored by the bones, we switched. Mike sat down to delve deeper into the fly box looking for a solution, and I moved to the bow.

The school moved around the corner of the island to some shallow water and Cassidy poled us over. They were milling around, certainly not the aggressive tailing and feeding we wanted to see, but at least they seemed fairly content. The winds were not terribly heavy, but there was a breeze and it was straight into my face. The fish were maybe fifty feet out.

I powered a cast into the wind to the right edge of the school, and stripped it back slowly. No takers. I laid another cast into the front edge of the school, and as I stripped it back they casually ignored it and moved a little further off. I pulled a little more line off my reel and laid a cast slightly to the left of where I thought they were. We waited. There were maybe thirty fish in the school, but they could mystically vanish in water that barely deep enough to cover their backs. We waited.

I thought I glimpsed a couple of fish cruise over a sandy spot, in the direction of my fly. At the same time Cassidy saw the main body of school reappear, cruising toward us. Dark torpedo shaped silhouettes gliding over the bottom, as clear as day. "Strip it in and take a shot at them," motioning toward the leading edge of school coming at us.

I stripped once and on the second, resistance. The live, vivid resistance I longed for. A few fish had moved over my fly; what I had glimpsed was not a product of optimism and too many hours staring at the water, from which copious schools of bonefish can spring, but the real thing.

The fish exploded across the flat, first headed left, away from the island. Line jumped off the deck and through the guides, and perhaps the most terrifying moment in fly fishing, when loose line is flying around boat parts, toes, buttons on sleeves, rod buts, reel handles, and any number of other protrusions that could catch it and, in an instant, cause the fragile tippet to part, was over almost before it had begun. I had him on the reel, and it started to whir, but only for an instant. He changed direction and headed at breakneck speed back to the island. It was bizarre and it had the feel of impending doom. Not so much for my hopes of landing a decent bonefish, but for the fish itself. It was like watching a boat speeding full-bore at a sandbar: you could not turn away and anticipated injury. Saltwater rode up the fly line, spraying a trail across our bow. The fish seemed intent on beaching himself, and furiously I banged the rim of my spool to make it spin, trying to keep tension on the line.

Upon reaching the shore, the fish whirled around, apparently rethinking its plan of making it a land-battle, and raced back out. As luck would have it, or perhaps and the fish planned it, the landward loop had taken the line around a mangrove. I saw and comprehended what had happened and I braced for the seemingly inevitable premature parting of ways between my bonefish and me. But, it was a lonely young mangrove shoot, and it was pliable. As the bone surged, the mangrove yielded, bending toward him, bending further, and then leaning back against him. My line was firmly around the mangrove, but I could still feel the fish. The mangrove, once thought to be a dreaded pitfall in my fish fight, was now an able, if unreliable, accomplice.

A sage and simple piece of fly-fishing advice I picked up somewhere is to always, when conditions allow, fly fish barefoot. When you are barefoot and standing on your line, you know it, whereas in sneakers, sandals, flats boots, or any kind of other footwear, you can be cheerfully and unknowingly stomping all over your line, ruining many casts and even breaking off a few fish. And now, I stood barefoot on the bow.

"I am going in," I said, planning to hop over, run around the mangrove, and reestablish a direct line to my fish. I gave little thought to the potential dangers underfoot, which I quickly deemed would be less damaging than losing the fish.

A split second before I jumped from the boat, Cassidy stopped me, taking note of my bare feet.

"Don't, there are sharp rocks down there," he said, and before any further discussion, he was over the side in his boots moving swiftly toward the mangrove. He looped wide around my fish to avoid sending him into a panic and further putting my fragile tippet in jeopardy. He reached the mangrove.

"Get ready to strip when I free it," he said. I was one step ahead of him, holding my rod high, ready to gain the inevitably loose line by stripping in quick six-foot swaths rather than inch-by-inch as I cranked the reel.

Cassidy flipped the line off the mangrove, I stripped, and the bonefish shot left over the flat again. Much depleted, perhaps in will as much as in strength, his run stopped short, if just short, of the backing. He turned, yielding to the drag, and I started to gain on him slowly. I had him coming in fairly steadily, but he circled the boat, and I had to hold my rod up over the push pole anchoring us the sand, and make my way around the boat with him. Eventually, I had him back at the bow, and though he had some nerve wracking spurts left in when he came close, it wasn't long before Cassidy, who had made it back aboard, had the leader, and shortly thereafter, the fish in his hand. Clearly, Cassidy's help disqualified it as an official catch by any official rulebook, and just as clearly, it has no adverse effects on my feelings about the catch. I often say that the difference between zero and one fish is a lot more than the difference between one and ten. In Guanaja it took two fish, but now I have some kind of measurable success, and I will rest a little easier.

Later in the day, Mike landed a bonefish, his first. It came from a mudding school in slightly deeper water, perhaps not the quintessential bonefish experience ever, but exciting nonetheless. I suppose Mike's luck, between the pulled hook and the jacks, has been even worse than mine this trip, and for him to get the target species was a relief. It was exciting, there were a couple schools of bonefish and a few permit cruising around the area. Occasionally they would make a mud, and occasionally we would sight the schools themselves cruising through the water column. It was exciting, visual fishing. Cassidy directed Mike and me to shoot casts in all directions around the boat as he caught glimpses of the fish. After Mike got his bonefish, I had an exciting take on a Kung-Fu Crab, and for a moment we all thought permit, but after short time it was clear it was a small bonefish. I had a fish on the line that we had come thousands of miles for, a fish that had been exceedingly difficult to come by all week, and upon realizing that, we were all a little disappointed.

I awoke today to a beautiful morning. Light winds, with plenty of east in them. During lunch Wednesday, Cassidy mentioned that permit often cruised the north side of island at dawn, right along the beautiful sandy shore over which our balcony looked. It lends itself very well to having one guy with a rod patrolling the beach, and another staying in the balcony to take advantage of the tremendous and uninhibited birds eye view of a big chunk of the beach, and directing the angler on the beach to the fish. It is not a strategy we have utilized to this point, mostly because we have not seen too many fish along the stretch, and devoting a spotter to an area that has not proven to consistently hold fish, at least during our stay, seemed counterproductive. Regardless though, the mention of permit was more than enough to get me out of bed with a rod. I told Mike my plan, and he said he would meet me at breakfast in a little while.

I took my rod and walked the shore, scanning the water for a skinny black sickle fin: the start of so many fishing dreams. At home, many of my most fervent and persistent dreams and recurring visions centered around the skinny black sickle tail of white marlin, waving and flipping across the surface, in a lackadaisical manner that contradicts the streamlined, powerful and agile beauty it is attached to. Here I was, a few thousand miles away, scanning water, a few feet deep rather than a hundred and twenty, for another thin, black wisp of a tail breaking the surface. A tail attached to a fish of perhaps thirty pounds, or even larger, though I would be happy with six. In any case diminutive compared to the sickle tailed white marlin perhaps approaching one hundred pounds, but just as sturdy and able foundation for big dreams. A flats permit, the fly-rodders' ultimate prize, a major accomplishment, rare and unlikely, challenging, and perhaps awaiting me there on that beach in front of my room at Graham's. I walked and looked, shortly reaching the dock, perhaps a couple hundred yards away at most, planning to devote some time scanning the home flat where we consistently saw bones, and yesterday, a big permit. During my four minute walk, the weather swiftly deteriorated. High winds rose and thick, dark clouds covered the sky. Even if a permit were present, seeing it became a near impossibility, and the wind was more than enough to make fly casting a comedy of errors.

I returned to the room and then shuffled off to the bar with my rod and fly box, intending to eat breakfast and then sit at the bar drinking coffee until a suitable window opened for me to resume my search for fish, which would happily and more likely include bonefish.

***

Sitting here at the bar drinking more coffee, contemplating Mangrove Cay, Miami, Puerto Rico, and a five day beating here, I can not help but wonder about the possibility of some kind of curse. The examination calls for a look at both sides, and before I can get too far into thinking I am a victim of more than my share of bad luck, days are remembered when things came together just as I wished. There probably has never been more on the line for fishing trips in terms of return on investment than when three of my friends and my brother accompanied me to Costa Rica in lieu of the traditional bachelor party. John Brennan met us at the airport, and after introductions, I asked, "So we are here regardless now, how is the fishing?"

"Well, there are a ton of dolphin around, but sailfishing hasn't been great, last week we raised two sails in three days" he replied, and as our collective hope plummeted, he added, "but the moon changed a couple days ago, we haven't fished since, and I think some fish may have come in with it," leaving us with at least some hope to sleep on. We headed out the next morning. My buddy Toph, my brother and I were fishing with John and my buddies Paul and Jim were on another boat with

Captain Keith. We put out our spread and started trolling, Toph insisting that I take the first fish to show him how it was done, and my brother demurring because he had no strong will to catch fish anyhow. He was along out of brotherly love, best man responsibility, and to do some drinking on boats in warm weather. After about four minutes of trolling, a ballyhoo got eaten off a long rigger. I figured it was a dolphin, their consistent presence being described further by both John and Keith the night before as reaching the level of nuisance, but I dropped it back for a while, locked it up, and a sailfish immediately took to the air. We all whooped with joy, and within minutes, we had our first release. Within the hour, Toph and my brother had both released sailfish as well. They had moved in for our arrival, our timing had been superb. My buddy Paul caught a blue marlin that day on the other boat, and over the three days I believe we released forty-eight sails, enough dolphin that, though none of us was ready to call them a nuisance, we could at least get a feel for where Keith and John were coming from, a wahoo for Toph, and a couple little yellowfin.

This past summer, at the start of our tuna hot streak, there were some decent reports about the southern chunk of Crab Ledge, and some decent reports of fish further out near the BC buoy. I put in our lines near Crab Ledge and trolled toward the BC, hoping to encounter fish somewhere. After about twenty minutes of trolling east, we got our first bite and shortly thereafter, our first fish. I trolled in lazy circles and figure eights around the weighpoint where we got that first bite for three days, getting seventeen more bites without ever going more than two miles away from the first bite. Fog was persistent on those three days, and spotting the whales and the birds and the life to lead you to the fish was impossible, but that first hook-up was a stroke of early good fortune, and it produced three fantastic days.

When I was twenty, I was invited by Wayne Whippen to fish giants with him onboard his sportfisher *Tighline*, which at the time was a Viking. We fished two consecutive days, departing the Nantucket Boat Basin in the pre-dawn darkness. The first day Wayne caught and released three fish, all too short (rats, as they are known when in pursuit of giants). All three were around 150lbs, rats to seasoned giant fishermen and highly prized by me. After the third fish of the morning, Wayne said it was my turn, and the bite abruptly shut off, as it often does tuna fishing. But I was invited along the next morning, and I would be in the chair first. We arrived to very thick fog and we put out the spread. I recall a debate going on between Wayne, his captain, and his mate, about the fishiness of the spot, and the difficulties in finding fish in the fog, and I saw a tuna jump out of the water next to the boat.

"A tuna just jumped right there," I said, and they turned in time to see the splash.

"Are you sure it wasn't a porpoise or a whale?" somebody asked.

And I said, "No, I saw it, is was a definitely a tuna." I think Wayne had faith enough in me to believe I could distinguish a tuna from a dolphin or a whale with a high degree of accuracy, but the captain and mate eyed me skeptically and looked like they were trying to decide whether to believe me or not. About four seconds later, another one, or perhaps even the same one, blew up on the spreader bar just off the transom and as line screamed off the Tiagra 130, a lot more weight was given to my original sighting. I hopped in the chair and happily fought what I considered the best fish of my life to that point. It was not the biggest, I had wrestled in some larger blue sharks, but they certainly don't have the cache of bluefin, and a 150 pounder was just fine with me. Just like the previous day, we got two more bites in quick succession, and I happily reeled in all three fish.

Also along for the ride that day was a somewhat elderly gentleman. Wayne told me and the crew that if we got another small one, the old guy should give it a shot in the chair, but if we got a "real" bite, then I should get back in the chair. The bite shut off anyhow, just as it had the morning before. We trolled around for several more hours, the fog burned off shortly after the fish turned off, and it was pretty nice day offshore. In the early afternoon, the determination was made to head in, and I was heading home happy.

We hadn't steamed west toward Nantucket for long, when the throttles came back down, and we were told to get the lines back out. There was a school of giants on the surface. Maybe ten or twenty fish, cruising along, their second dorsal fins moving up and down in the water, much like dolphins. The lines went back out, and they were dragged in front of the pack. Two fish could be seen to move with an urgency, though whether it was an urgency born of hunger or avoidance of danger remained in doubt for just a moment, until one of lines popped from the rigger.

I was pretty sure the fish were big, but I didn't want to steal the old guy's turn, so I waited. Wayne and company quickly yelled at me to get in the chair. A bluefin of 150 pounds is capable of quite a fight, but with a bent-butt 130, in a chair with a harness, the fights were short-lived, maybe ten minutes. After ten minutes, and after twenty, this fish was still making moves rather quickly away from the boat. I fought it for a little more than an hour, which seemed like four, and eventually, I had it to the boat. A gaff was produced, but after a short debate, a harpoon was produced too. On the first shot with the harpoon, the captain missed. Wayne and the mate asked him how he managed to miss something the size of a Volkswagon as the reinvigorated tuna dashed away from the boat again. I worked it back in, and this time, the captain connected with the harpoon. The fish took off and I reeled him in again, but the harpoon had

174

taken a lot out of the fish and a lot out of the drama of the fight. He came to boat, got tail-roped to back, and I had my first giant. It weighed 525 pounds, and was another shining example of some excellent timing on the water.

Lastly, I think of another recent vacation, not even my own vacation, but another of Bill Palmer's. For years, during our weeks in August, we always tossed around the possibility of Bill coming back in the spring for some flats fishing, or in the fall for albacore. After the strong bite of 2011, our radar for an albacore trip was really up this past fall. Annie Fey caught Nantucket's first one of the year with me on the Bonito Bar, not long after Bill departed in August. On day one of the Nantucket Slam early in September we caught nine. I called Bill and left a message. I said it was pretty good, and he should probably get back the next weekend. He called back, and said the upcoming weekend was no good, but he would pencil in the next one. I said sure, and said I would call him in a week and half or so, and give him an update, but I feared the fickle albies would depart and we would miss our window. But as the time passed, albacore fishing got better and better. Then we got the weather report for the penciled in weekend, and it was no good. Strong wind and rain and we said we would try the next weekend. I thought it was going to be the end of it. The albies would scurry south with the bad weather, and while Mike and I had already had a banner season, Liz had gotten her first and added a couple more, Bill would miss out. When the rain stopped, and wind laid down, the albies remained, and the next weekend, a full three and half weeks after I originally called and said hurry to Nantucket for the albacore bite, he came in. I picked him up at the airport and we raced downtown, and took the *Topspin* up to Great Point to catch the east tide. Great Point looked dead as we drove by, but some birds worked the Galls, and a few casts with Deadly Dicks netted a few albacore, and not long after the trip had begun it was a success. We headed back to Great Point and found fish blitzing just north of the edge, where we caught several more. Bill had some shots with a fly rod, but didn't connect, and we drove back home into the setting sun. We ate a typically excellent dinner at the Club Car and had a happy and restful night sleep, knowing we had accomplished the trip's goals in the first couple hours on the first afternoon and everything from here on was gravy. We headed to Madaket in the morning, met Mike, and motored out to start our routine of drifting out the cut on the tide, waiting for shots. We did not have to wait long. Bill got into another on a Deadly Dick and I got one on the fly on our first drift out. I handed the fly rod to Mike for the next drift, and he got one on the fly and Bill connected again with the spinner. Then we all started fly fishing and it wasn't long before Bill added one on the fly. The blitzes became bigger, more fish seemed to join each group of blitzing fish on each drift. Then they started to last longer, the surface continually churned and boiled for minutes and minutes on end. Every drift was productive, many with fly rod doubles. We started to see the electric green backs of albies surfing the standing waves around the cut. A fly in their vicinity was savagely pounced on without hesitation. We spent way more time fighting fish than we did casting.

At the time, I realized I was in midst of something special, I think we all did, but we did not think about it too much. For one thing, there was the superstitious type of nervousness, like talking about a no-hitter. We knew were in the midst of something remarkable and if we said anything, it may vanish. But even more than that, we were just flat out busy catching fish. Every time one was landed, there were either more fish to cast to immediately, or huge busting pods to drive around and drift through again.

It kept getting better and better. Our final half hour seemed like one continuous blitz, and then we wrapped it up. The tide was dying, and the fishing seemed to be slowing down a little bit: that is to say there were only about a dozen pods of breaking fish and they seemed to actually be going down for short periods of time, and Bill needed to hop on a plane and get home. Nobody counted how many we got. We were not out to break any records, win any tournaments or keep any tallies. I would guess that we each got somewhere north of ten albacore on the fly, but if it was seven the day would not lose anything, nor would it gain anything if we got twenty. Given some time to reflect on it, some time to think about it, the grandeur and perfection of the day have only grown. To pick a single greatest day of fishing from amongst a lifetime of great days fishing is probably a foolish task, but when the thought does cross my mind, that day is quickly remembered. And the thought of that day vanquishes any thought that I have been afflicted by some curse. Bill had about a twenty-four hour window of fishing time, and while I had plenty of windows that fall, having Bill in town ensured that I would be on the water, and during that short window, we had the best albacore fishing of our lives. Luck and fate and whatever else conspired to push that trip back a full three weeks past when it was supposed to happen, past when I *recommended* it happen, to get us to the Madaket cut on that day, where their were more hungry albacore than I thought I would ever see in a whole season, maybe a whole lifetime.

***

Graham's Place isn't really on the island of Guanaja, but on its own private cay. The cay is one of many and they form a barrier reef. Our balcony overlooks a sandy flat which drops off into a sound, and on the opposite shore mountains rise rapidly into the sky. I look out over them every night before I go to sleep. It is nice to be in the warm air, nice to be near a beach with a fly rod and have no further agenda. Given my roots along the eastern seaboard of the United States, I am not sure I will ever get used to mountains covered in tropical flora rising straight up out of the ocean. This is exactly the kind of place that could make an expat out of me. Instead of having all of the

177

above for a week, I would have them for months, or for years. We are at a hotel and it is not costing us all that much. If I got a cheap rental, ate at home, and was otherwise slightly frugal, I could make it work. In fact, I probably would if I were still single. I would forget about finding a job in sportfishing for the winter, I would fish all summer, scallop until it got tough, and then be on a flight out toward wadeable flats for a duration of months not days.

These thoughts all rattle around in my head as I look out from the balcony over a view and a landscape that would look the part if labeled "paradise," but these are not the thoughts foremost on my mind. I think about Chick going to bed, or hopefully already sleeping, two thousand miles away. I think about Liz and how she is doing. I hope Chick is making her smile, I hope she is having fun with him, I hope she is having fun with her mother. I do not really miss reading Chick stories at night. He does not seem to enjoy *The Story of Ferdinand* as much as I do, and he usually chooses books I do not particularly enjoy, but I sure do miss being with him when he chooses them. I miss him saying, "No, Dadda, not *Ferdinand*," showing immense patience with me, and exclaims "these," as he piles books about building roads in my lap. I miss giving him a hug and kiss and putting him in his crib and then going to join Liz in our bed, to talk and laugh for a little while before falling asleep.

It is inevitable that I spend a chunk of my time at home wishing I were fishing somewhere warm, and equally inevitable that when I am fishing somewhere warm I spend a chunk of it wishing I were with Liz and Chick. I take some comfort in knowing they will be there and happy to see me when I get home, and even more comfort knowing I am a very loved, very lucky man, which more than makes up for the fact I will not be living in hut on the beach with my fly tackle for the next couple months. I head inside to bed trying to think of the fish just outside the door. Being where you are, and not spending too much time wishing you were elsewhere, is the only consistently effective tactic to maximize happiness as a fishing nut navigating family life.

***

Friday, my thirty-second birthday, and our last day, our last chance. For the first time, I had Mike set his alarm for five. Before bed I prepared my rod, an eight weight on the stout side, with a reel given to me by my wife as a wedding present, which has spent the majority of the trip as my designated permit rod. I had tied on a new tippet and a Kung Fu Crab.

I got out of bed with the alarm and looked out off the balcony. Birthday wishes for a calm, sunny day were immediately dashed, at least for the foreseeable future. Fairly strong winds and cloudy skies. Regardless, I headed out, the alternatives being more sleep, or diving back into Tom Wolfe's *Back to Blood*, both of which would be at least theoretically available back home, whereas bonefish and permit would not.

I walked the beach, with my rod and Kung Fu Crab, scanning intently, focused on a stretch of patchy grass bottom maybe ten yards offshore where I suspected permit may cruise. I made it to the dock, scanning the flat on the other side of it, and turned back. Walking back, still scanning ten yards offshore for the thin black sickle of dreams, I bumbled onto four bonefish. They were cruising tight to the shore, very tight, and I was on top of them before I saw them. When I looked down, practically at my feet, there they were. But in the early morning light, they did not seem affected by my presence and the continued to move along the beach. I cut off my Kung Fu Crab with my teeth and chose a light weight creation inspired by the Avalon Permit fly, a modification of my own, dreamed up at the fly tying desk in Nantucket, thousands of miles from bonefish and permit, and, as far as I know, never tested or proven on the bonefish of the world. But at this point, it was time for something new, and this fly wasn't really much of a departure from accepted bonefish patterns: some brownish-tan rabbit hair, a little orange tuft, and little burnt mono eyes.

I walked around the fish and flicked my fly the length of the leader from the shore. One of the fish swam toward it. I gave it a little twitch, and he raced toward it. He eyed it intently and I gave it another two twitches. My week of previous experience conditioned me to expect that he would soon turn away and be gone. Much to my surprise the little fella swam a little more, and then sucked it into his mouth. I was awed, perplexed, amazed and astounded. I couldn't strip-set, because I had no line left to strip, the entire incident was taking place at the end of my rod tip. In hindsight, what the situation called for was spastically raising the rod, a maneuver all my good fishing instincts went against.

And then it was over. As quickly as the little guy had sucked up my fly, he spit it out. Certainly, in moments like that, when a fish much desired is somehow lost or missed, one tends to analyze it: wondering what could have been done differently, replaying the events, criticizing your own actions, perhaps at great length. Lost fish have in the past haunted my thoughts for months, but I will not beat myself up over that little guy. I am not even sure the seemingly appropriate spastic and immediate raising of my rod tip would have got him.

I stood at the shore, more than a little amazed and a little disappointed, but for the most part, taking the encounter as a good sign of things to come. Perhaps the bonefish en masse had finally got hungry.

Then the weather deteriorated quickly, and I took my rod to the bar to drink coffee, once again.

13

Ode to Florida
Daydreams of a Father

In a few months, Chick, his mother, and his grandmothers are headed off to Disney World. I will be working and I will not be going along, but it will not bother me to miss the Magic Kingdom. Liz has been dreaming of this trip, probably since well before Chick's birth. It will be his first trip to the Sunshine State, and in all likelihood, his first of many, because I too dream of introducing him to Florida, though the Florida I want to show him is quite different. On future family trips to Disney (of which I have advised Liz that my lifetime quota is two and she should use them cautiously), I intend to get away as much as possible to the Mosquito Lagoon and surrounding waters in pursuit of redfish and whatever else may be available. In fact, if the ratio is favorable in terms of time with a rod to time in theme park lines, she may even be able to get more than two trips out of me. Chick may get his first taste of the different Florida on one of those trips by suggesting he would like to accompany me, in search of fish, instead of another day in the theme parks. Maybe it will be later, once he has grown out of theme parks all together, but hopefully someday, he will want me to show him a little bit of the Florida I love.

I went to Disney World once when I was little kid too, but the trip where I fell in love with Florida came when I was in middle school. I walked outside the airport doors in Miami, surprised and delighted at the hot night air outside. My Dad drove the rental car south and I peered from the back seat at the palm trees along the highways, and for the first time anywhere other than on Nantucket, I considered that this was a place where perhaps I belonged. I was filled to the brim with fishing information gleaned from guidebooks and magazines. I knew that snook, and even tarpon, liked brackish backwaters and as we drove, I had the urge to stop and cast into every roadside puddle and drainage ditch we passed, just about certain there were large gamefish lurking in each of them.

Our destination was Islamorada and upon arrival I found myself in my first true "fishing town." There is plenty of fishing in Nantucket, but it is a town dominated by quaintness, luxury and history. Its atmosphere is still influenced more by the whaling done a century and a half ago than by any sportfishing done today. Islamorada is a town that lives and breathes fishing. Instead of one charter boat dock, like Nantucket, this tiny island had several, one marina after another. Big sportfishers lined up against the ocean side of US 1, and flats skiffs along the backcountry side, with plenty more under the covered roof at Holiday Isle. It seemed every other store was a tackle shop, the streets were named for fish, fish mounts were everywhere, and a Guy Harvey t-shirt seemed to be the local uniform. For a boy who lived and breathed fishing, it certainly topped Disney World.

I went on to have the unsuccessful sailfish trip on the dubious boat, and an equally unsuccessful bonefish trip. My parents sent my brother and me out with an old guide, who stopped the boat every few minutes to pee. It was windy, and we snaked through the mangroves and popped out on a little flat behind an island and he began to chum with shrimp chunks. We threw little jigs tipped with shrimp into the chum. We were supposed to slowly bounce and retrieve the jigs along the bottom, but for some reason we lost a considerable number of the jigs. Now, with a little more experience under my belt, I still wonder why our jigs were in such peril on that little bonefish flat. Perhaps there was some jagged coral on the bottom, but in any case, jigs were lost and the guide did not appreciate it. To say that he was not child friendly would not be a stretch. Once a barracuda bit off a jig, so from that point on, whenever my brother or I lost a jig, we would turn around for a new one and say, "Sorry, barracuda" because a barracuda was unavoidable whereas it seemed that the other invisible jig pitfall was avoidable, or so the guide's mood suggested.

We did hook a few bonefish. I remember the guide enthusiastically telling (yelling at) my brother and me to stop reeling against the drag. At the onset of your sportfishing career, somebody needs to explain drags to you. The Northeast is a region fond of heavy tackle, even more so then than today, and it is possible for a boy growing up here to get through his early fishing years never comprehending drag, the reel being a device for retrieving line. If a fish was taking line off your reel, well, you just cranked down on the drag until it stopped so you could start pumping up and reeling down on him again. And especially, when it comes to children, people have a tendency to encourage them to "just crank"- the subtleties of drag can be explained later, but for now lets get the fish in. At the time of this trip, I knew drag existed, but I was still a little vague on the actual workings. Apparently, we were reeling against the drag a bit, and the guide, perhaps because of the significant loss of jigs, did not want to see unnecessary wear and tear on his reels, told us to stop. At first, I bristled a little bit, taking advice not being a particular strong suit of mine. After briefly thinking that I didn't need reeling advice from this guy, I gave him a look that said, "Well, if I knew what the hell you were talking about, I would give it a shot." He explained briefly, that by reeling when the fish was trying to take line, I wasn't doing any good and I was just twisting up the line, and the reel was making a funny noise. If I heard the noise, stop cranking. It was not the most touching educational scene, a gruff cranky guide instructing a pain-in-ass know-it-all kid, but it was in fact educational, and certainly the last time I reeled against the drag. At some point during the trip, I hooked and fought a large Islamorada bonefish to the boat, where it was lost. I blamed the loss of the fish solely on the guide, and his lack of a net or failure to use a net. Looking back, though, I suppose it is possible that, as a kid who didn't know enough to not reel against the drag, perhaps my fish fighting and movements near the boat where not as smooth as they could have been and I played a role in the fish's premature release. In any case, that was as close as we got to a bonefish all day.

I returned to Nantucket, not a newly crowned angling champion with multiple releases of many tropical species, including billfish and bonefish, but with one large barracuda to show for my efforts. Luckily, a barracuda plays pretty well in middle school, a lot better than it does in fishing bars, and I wasn't the target of ridicule amongst my peers.

Our family vacations from then on always produced some debate. My mother wanted to be somewhere warm and preferably on a beach; my father and brother needed activities, usually golf; and I wanted to fish. My mother would have preferred the southern Caribbean, actually preferring it hot to just warm and not wanting to take any chances being that the vacation was usually in February. My father, in addition to wanting to hit the links, is and was finicky about temperature. He wants it neither too hot nor too cold, preferring a comfortable golfing temperature of around sixty-seven to seventy-four degrees, and his first choice would probably have been Hilton Head, Central Florida or the West Coast of Florida where golf courses abound and it didn't get too hot. He expressed naked terror when my mother casually floated out

Mexico, Aruba, or other hot spots. My brother, in addition to golfing with our Dad, enjoyed go-carts, and he seemed happy to go anywhere if there would be a trip or preferably trips to ride go-carts or other motorized attractions.

Of course, inspired by my reading in *Saltwater Sportsman* and other periodicals, I recommended vacations totally beyond the pale. I was firm in my belief that my parents should pack us all off to Panama's Tropic Starr, the Golfito Sailfish Rancho, or other remote and expensive fishing lodges with little to offer anybody but the devout angler.

Many times, this led to a family vacation to Florida, and sometimes it was a split trip between the West Coast and the Keys. On the West Coast, my father could golf and my brother could drive go-carts, or on one occasion, spend the vast majority of his time at a driving range with a hokey carnival-esque challenge paying cash for shots close to a pin on a floating green. I forget the specifics, but the odds certainly were not good. I believe the shots were expensive and the payout was graduated based on consecutive excellent shots. It would have cost my parents a fortune, but my brother had it dialed in. He was up a few hundred at one point, and had rolled a shot at a ten-thousand-dollar hole-in-one across the rim, which was all too much to fathom for an eleven-year old.

In the Keys, there was at least a decent chance at my mother getting a couple beach days, and I could fish. Certainly, I could have enjoyed some of the West Coast's world-class fishing too, but I always saved my fishing for the Keys, hoping for sailfish, bonefish and tarpon.

One day in the Keys, we rented a boat. While my father and brother never cared too much about the fishing, they did, and do, love boats. My father arranged the boat the day before, and all three of us looked forward to the next day with giddy excitement, perhaps a rarity on a trip where interests did not collide. I did not think we were up to finding tarpon or bonefish, so barracuda was the target species, and we got a good location from a local tackle store. Covering some ground, seeing some sights, and lunch at a boat-up restaurant were priorities for my father and brother. It was before GPS, and we spent that night in the hotel with a chart, plotting our course, writing down the channel markers and landmarks and what course for how long would get us to the next one, and mapped out our whole day from barracuda, to lunch a few Keys down, and back home again.

We didn't even get a barracuda, though I did have a couple followers and one strike, which I missed, but it didn't matter. Finding the barracuda was victory in and of itself, but more to the point, it was just a great day with my Dad and brother and the memory lingers decades later.

Once I was off to college and not in the vacation debate anymore, the trips shifted purely to Florida's West Coast, the golfing and go-carting there being superior to that of the Keys, and my mother, now outnumbered two-to-one, was left out in the cold literally and figuratively. Shortly thereafter, my father bought a small place on Pine Island, outside of Fort Myers. Perfectly situated near some golfing, but even more so, a perfect home base for messing about in boats.

When my college career was coming to a close, and I began to look at law schools, I really considered only two. When choosing a college I had made my decision based on academic reputation, courses of study, class size, and things of that nature, things that guidance counselors and parents encourage you to consider. I ended up at Drew University in New Jersey, and I loved my time there, but my priorities shifted a little bit in my search for a law school. The writing may have been on the wall as far as a career in law, given that job placement, national ranking, average LSAT scores, and all that stuff took a distinct back seat to the availability of fish and specifically billfish. The University of Miami and the University of Hawaii comprised my entire list. I applied and was accepted to Miami. At the time it was about the highest ranked school I could hope to gain acceptance to, significantly above any school in Boston where I had a chance of admission, and that seemed a nice selling point to my folks. As far as they were concerned, it sure beat Hawaii. It beat Hawaii for me too, Florida having held a part of my heart ever since that first ride down to Islamorada in middle school.

I lived in Miami for three years, fishing harder than I studied, and to be honest, partying at least as hard as I did either. Steve Campbell, a friend of my uncle's who I had met on a fishless yet excellent bonefish trip to Bimini, had a condo at Ocean Reef and a Contender. He would come down weekends and needed somebody to go fishing with him, and I was just the guy to do it. I would drive down from Miami in predawn darkness, sometimes with a buddy or two, get let through the gates of the prestigious club as a guest of Mr. Campbell's and we would fish.

After the unsuccessful sailfish trip on my first trip to the Keys, I probably went on a minimum of a half dozen more sailfish trips over the years, all with knowledgeable (or allegedly knowledgeable) charter captains, and all in decent places. The Keys, Fort Lauderdale, Miami, and never, did we so much as hook a sailfish. I was desperate to get some billfish experience and it was not coming easy.

On my first trip with Steve, and my good friend, Jake Forgit, who was visiting at the time, fishing the reef off Key Largo, slow trolling live ballyhoo, I got one. A pack of little dolphin came through our spread and we got one of them but they chewed up every bait. We went to work putting out new ballyhoo. Almost immediately after we got them back out, one got eaten, and line flowed from the spool; we all figured the dolphin were still around. I took the rod, engaged the drag, and a large Atlantic sailfish started dancing across the surface as line tore off the reel. Several excruciating minutes later, we had him

187

at the boat. He tail-wrapped himself on his last jump, and as I worked him those final yards, I was terrified the line would chafe on him enough to part, and he would be gone. Thankfully though, Jake grabbed him by the tail, we scooped him, unwrapped him, and sent him back overboard. My first billfish, and a fine morning.

During my last year of law school I worked on a charter boat out of Miami Beach Marina, as a mate and sometimes a captain. I learned a ton, and thoroughly enjoyed a little taste of professional sailfishing, getting enough experience with billfish to be able to rest a little easier at night.

Many weekends I would head to my Dad's place on Pine Island. At first, I was disappointed he got a place on the west coast, away from sailfish, but a place to lay my head and boat was more than enough to get me across Alligator Alley. Pine Island is a pretty easy place for an angler to fall in love with, and it did not take me long. As my appreciation for flats and shallows grew to rival my enthusiasm for billfish, my adoration of Pine Island grew right along with it. I have fished Pine Island more now than anywhere except Nantucket, redfish and snook are amongst my favorite species, and I look forward to every trip back.

During the day I spent bonefishing with Rich Smith in Miami when it was slightly too cold, amongst many other things, we talked about his favorite kind of fishing. Immediately, I recognized in Rich (as he recognized in me) that he was the kind of nut who went fishing on his days off from over three hundred days of guiding a year. Given his proximity to so many species, so many methods, so many spots, I wondered what he liked to do most, what he would fish for on his days off? Without hesitation he replied tarpon. He said tarpon season is his favorite, tarpon fishing his forte. He advised that I beg, borrow, and steal to get back and fish with him during tarpon season.

I regard this type of advice very highly. Find a guide, not just somebody deluded enough to think it is a moneymaking proposition, but a true fishing nut, and ask them what they do on their days off. If they golf, you haven't found a true fishing nut, but if they fish, ask what kind of fishing do they do, and if possible, can you do it too? If the guide is doing it on his day off, it is probably the coolest thing going, maybe not the highest rate of success, maybe requiring a little extra skill or a little extra patience, but whatever the risk, it is worth consideration. This case, experiencing the fabled tarpon migration in the Florida Keys, did not require that I go out on a limb to put my trust in Rich. Everybody knows Florida in the spring is the place to be for legendary tarpon fishing, but hearing Rich talk about it moved it quickly up my fishing wish list. At the end of the day he showed me *Riding High: A Season on Fly*, a short movie for which he had guided the anglers and producers for a number of days. It is an extremely cool video, it was shared all over the internet, and as far as I can tell, had the entire fly-fishing world drooling about a spring chasing tarpon in Florida. On the plane ride home from Florida, I was thinking about making it back.

It took me longer than I would have liked, but I made it. Liz and I headed to Florida a year and a half later for school vacation in late April. I emailed Rich and said I couldn't do May or June, due to school and an unwillingness to leave Nantucket, but I could do late April, and arrangements were made. To my delight, Liz fell in love with Pine Island on the first trip when we were dating, and jumps at the chance to go back. We spent a couple days there, one of which we fished with local guide Matt Mitchell, another true fishing nut.

I met Matt on one of my first trips down, he owed my Dad a favor for one thing or another, and we fished together. I have fished with him every chance since, sometimes having some buddies in town and needing another boat, usually once a trip these days for some consistent action I can not replicate, and occasionally if I am in town I get the coveted phone call to accompany him gratis on a scouting mission. Liz said we didn't need a guide this time down, and she just wanted to relax on the boat. But on day two she complained about the fishing, claiming she was ready for some catching, and I called Matt. Luckily, he was available for the next day, and we headed out. At our first stop Liz threw a live whitebait where Matt pointed. It hit that water and a snook hammered it. It was a touch and go battle, with the fish making a strong bid for the mangroves on two separate occasions, but Liz held it out both times. A real beauty around seventeen pounds, and her vacation was made, at least fishing-wise (which she still erroneously argues is only one factor of many in determining the success of vacation).

Shortly afterward we were headed down the Keys, at my behest, hoping to get into tarpon. I met Rich at his house on the designated morning in April, and we started out. On the first oceanside flat we checked, we saw two fish, but did not get a good shot. Rich seemed pleased with their presence. We looked and looked and looked, and for the rest of the morning and most of the afternoon we didn't see another fish. My eight hours came and went, but Rich was unwilling to give up on the day for another fishing nut like me, and perhaps felt some pressure being that he was the one that sold me on the trip to begin with. Rich declared that we were going to find some tarpon somewhere. I texted Liz to let her know there were no fish yet, and no end in sight. Sometime after five, we were somewhere in the backcountry, somewhere north of US 1. The light was low, and what was left of it was not helping our cause much because it was in our eyes, but Rich saw a couple fish. Then he saw a couple more, and they were headed toward us. I laid a cast out, waited a couple moments for his word, stripped, and bang, I had a tarpon. I set the hook vigorously, and the fish went to the air. Two jumps and a quick run, and then two more jumps. On the second, my fly fell from his mouth.

190

Rich was not concerned. The flat had come alive; there were groups of tarpon all over the place. He saw fish ahead and had me throw a cast as far as I could off the bow. After one strip, we both saw a lot of water move as a big fish moved for the fly with enthusiasm. I was on again, and again savagely set the hook, trying to do whatever I could to keep the fly in the fish's bony jaw. The first jump revealed the fish to be significantly larger than the first, well north of one hundred pounds, maybe 130.

I fought it for an hour. It pulled us quite a ways; we chased it quite a ways. At one point another school of tarpon starting busting bait beside the boat. It was hard to believe these were the same waters we had scoured all day looking for fish. Rich was giving me pointers on the fly in regards to wearing down big tarpon on the fly. I was exhausted *before* we hooked the fish. Finally, the leader clicked through the end of the rod: a catch. But our proximity to the fish was short lived, and it took off again. With nothing to lose now, except maybe a picture, I palmed the spool with all I had, trying to stop the behemoth. It slowed promisingly, but then it jumped, and the line went slack. Upon reeling in, we found the hook had broke, but regardless, we went home happy.

Liz was not thrilled with me. Our vacation weather woes continued to haunt us a little bit, it had been windy, cloudy and generally not conducive to pool lounging which is how she intended to spend the day. She was bored and hungry, my eight-or-so hour fishing trip having turned into about fourteen by the time Rich and I got back to the ramp and I got back to the hotel, but I was armed with a big fish story. It is hard to stay mad at a goofy exuberant angler, or least hard for Liz to stay mad at one, which is important given her choice of a life-partner.

The next day my buddy from law school, Zach Hicks, came down to fish with Rich and me. Having accomplished the tarpon on fly goal the day before, due to Rich's unwavering faith and perseverance, we decided on a more laid back approach. It was also a necessity that I be back on land by mid-afternoon, partially to travel home the next day, but more so to stay happily married. We checked a few tarpon spots, hit some mangroves, threw some plugs at big barracuda, and generally just had a good time out on the water. It was a great day, filled with fish and laughter. We spent some time around the Content Keys on flats as beautiful as any I have ever seen. That was the last time I was in Florida, but I will be back. The last hour of that long April day makes a strong case for the trip to be to the Keys in the spring, perhaps figure out how to make it May, taking the weather out of the equation just little bit more.

I spend plenty of time thinking about far-flung places, but our southernmost contiguous state supports more than its share of my daydreams. I think about a vacation rental on Summerland Key and some serious time around the Contents. It is hard to overlook Pine Island Sound, especially now that I have some experience there. The familiarity does not satisfy in the least, but only fuels the fire for more fishing, more exploring. Miami, home to my law school days, may offer the best metropolis fishing anywhere. The sight of a swordfish, my first and only, leaping out of the Gulfstream against the backdrop of a full-moon sky will forever be with me as a grand fishing moment. Florida, a state with enough fishing to last a lifetime and then some.

I hope Chick and his mom and grandmothers have a blast at Disney. I hope he laughs and smiles all day and passes out while his head is on its way to his pillow every night, happily exhausted from the spectacle of it all. I hope the trip is all Liz dreams it will be, and she will take the special delight that comes from seeing your child happy over and over again. Someday, probably not too soon, but someday, I hope to get the same delight from showing Chick Florida, from the mangroves to the

Gulfstream. I hope he passes out with his head on its way to the pillow, exhausted from a day in an angling paradise.

14

The Lost Fall

At some point in my mind, I started referring to it as the
"Lost Fall." Liz, Chick and I had moved. Not far, just up the
street, back into my childhood home. Not really my childhood
home actually, but where I stayed when I was home from college
and for a tense chunk of cohabitation in my twenties that many
American parents and children now endure. On top of the
move, I had calls for charters, and I started as a full time history
teacher at Nantucket's middle school.

I seemed extremely busy, a to-do list long enough to
keep me occupied for a decade, and yet, when thinking about it
now, in attempting to describe or prove just how busy I was,
there is nothing remarkable about it. Sure, I moved, and I had
some home improvement projects to take care of, but people
move all the time. I started a new job, even a new job that is
notoriously difficult the first year, but most people are employed.
And I had a wife and son who required care and attention, and
while they are remarkable, there is nothing remarkable about
spending time with your family. I was busy, even perhaps
particularly busy, but not to any extent that anybody else with a
job and a family and a couple more random obligations on top is
not familiar with. It was remarkable only to me, because I could
not, or did not, go fishing. My fishing trips were cut to tiny

sliver of what I would have liked, a mere fraction of what they once were.

There are the fishing trips I want to go on, and the fishing trips I need to go on. I do not mean I "need" to go because I have a client, I need to go on those too, but here I am speaking only of personal outings. Of the two, wanting to go is preferable. I fish because I have the time, because the fish are biting, because the tide coincides with sunrise, because somebody saw a couple white marlin twenty miles south, or any other number of good reasons. My soul receives a good deal of benefit from these outings even though it doesn't necessarily need it, like preventative maintenance and an oil change on an outboard.

Then there is going fishing because I need to go. An internal declaration is made, the product of dwindling patience and finely honed priorities, and I know I am not going to be much good to myself or to anybody else until I wet a line. There was not enough preventative maintenance and now my outboard seems sluggish and is making a troubling noise. That is the type of fishing I did this fall. A few times a month I would come to the conclusion that a few hours on Saturday or Sunday would be dedicated to fishing, more out of an instinct for self-preservation on the mental health front than anything else.

Boxes remained unpacked, things around the house remained unpainted or disassembled, and papers remained ungraded as I floated around looking for albies. I wanted to feel that jolt of resistance between my fingers as I stripped, and after seizing the line for a brief, but not too brief, moment to set the hook, I wanted to see and hear and feel the rubbery fly line jump off the deck and shoot through the guides as it followed the shimmering football blistering toward Martha's Vineyard. I wanted a taste of the bent fly rod, reel screaming excitement that permeated the last two falls to get me through the winter. I went out once with my Uncle Bob and once with Josh Eldridge. My uncle caught the only false albacore I witnessed being caught all fall, just a little south of Tuckernuck, casting a spinning rod to little pods of fish that would blitz briefly before disappearing. The next time I was on my way to Madaket, and on the spur of the moment, decided to try Josh. He was available, and happy to meet me in Madaket, though we didn't manage to catch a thing.

Both times, we were in the Madaket cut at the beginning of the outgoing tide. Both times there were fish blitzing. Little pods of them, and the blitzes didn't last long, but they were there. It had a good anticipatory feel. It was easy, in the optimistic mind of an angler, to imagine the little blitzes as just the tip of the iceberg. A little pod of fish start busting bait here and there at the beginning of the tide, and the tide flows a little harder and the fish blitz a little more often, and then another pod starts busting bait, and the pods seemingly grow and the blitzes last longer, until, it is just one continuous blitz by a seemingly endless school of fish. But such events, common in the dreams of anglers and in the fall of 2012, are far from guaranteed, and in 2013 the pods of albies never grew and the blitzes didn't last.

I had maybe two or three marginal shots with my fly rod in the two outings, and none resulted in a hook-up, or even a swing and a miss. I never picked up a spinning rod, perhaps at the cost of catching a false albacore in 2013, but in the end, going fishing was more important than catching anything.

I missed most of it, so I do not have good handle on the whole season, and on one hand, I am happy to go on believing that I did not miss much. A lost season in which the fish weren't biting anyway is not too bad. On the other hand, I am hoping that the spectacular albie bites of 2011 and 2012 are part of a general upswing with more and more great falls on the horizon, rather than an anomaly brought about by a rare cocktail of favorable conditions. From what I understand, there were some good tides, and good days, especially at Great Point. I got the sense that if I had been on the water every day, or even a few times a week, I could have ground out a respectable albie fall, but it would not have been terribly easy. That information is totally inconclusive, and I will interpret it as totally positive in that I didn't miss a world-class bite but they will be there next fall.

While false albacore have certainly headlined my last couple falls, they are not the only fishing option as the days grow shorter. Erik Passanante, Mike Brennan (a steady fishing companion of Erik's), Mike's brother-in-law, and I went offshore one Sunday in October and got a bluefin of about ninety pounds to end a lackluster recreational bluefin year on an up note, but the thirteen-hour fishing day left me with physical exhaustion to match my weary mental state. Mike Schuster enjoyed the most promising fall striper action in years, and I heard about stripers, both big and little, in the harbor into November, but I didn't pick a up a rod. The season ended with a reluctant period, rather than the bold exclamation point of previous years.

My shotgun remained locked in my gun cabinet for the entirety of the short October duck season. Deer season is only days away and instead of cleaned and recently sighted in, my deer rifle remains locked up and caked with some kind of yellow goop that is supposed to keep it pristine and corrosion-free in between deer seasons.

I am not much of a deer hunter anyway. To say the least, Nantucket is not a difficult place to shoot deer, and I have spent the last couple seasons sitting still in the woods bored out of my mind, occasionally listening to the gunshots of those around me who are better, better prepared, or just luckier. I spend about five percent of the time trying to convince myself that this quiet solitude in nature is wholesome self-improvement, and that shooting a deer isn't necessary for the experience to be worthwhile. For the remaining ninety-five percent of the time, my thoughts are divided evenly amongst where all the goddamn deer are, what I may be doing wrong, and pondering how cold I am, which is uniformly very, very cold. To sit this season out will not pain me too much.

If I do not liberate my shotgun from the gun cabinet and take it for a few walks during duck season, I will miss that more. Strolling through a marsh in the midst of winter, it is not a psychological challenge to convince myself that I am spending worthwhile time in nature. Nantucket's landscape is often at its most beautiful during the unpopulated months. The exercise keeps me warm, and the possibility of ducks exploding from the next puddle is excitement and enticement enough to keep the walk interesting. But if I don't get out, it will not wear on me too much. It will be nothing more than mounting responsibilities and allegedly sound priorities causing me to skip a potentially pleasant outing, whereas time off the water during fishing season seems like slow yet persistent erosion of my most cherished values and a clear and present danger to everything I hold sacred.

I think I adopted the idea of 2013 being my "lost fall" as a coping mechanism. Certainly, to lose a fall is not a pleasant thing. I would rather gain a fall, especially a fall with a good albie bite, but the alternative is far more grim. The alternative to a lost fall is that falls for the foreseeable future will be similar. If you ask a golfer if they got out much recently, they may reply, "No, I had knee surgery, I lost the whole season," and it is not good, but it is far preferable to, "Golf, boy, I wish I still had the time. Haven't gotten out like I used to in years."

To what end am I facing this terror? Why was my fall lost? To what do I fear further loss of falls, maybe springs, and perhaps even summers?

The fact that I have already navigated two falls as a father and did not declare either of them "lost" is troubling. Chick was around, though less mobile, for both spectacular albie seasons leading up to this one, and though I thought I should be fishing more at the time, I probably was fishing enough as evidenced by the fact that both falls stand out in my mind and on plenty of digital images (I was going to say film, but I am not old enough to start ignoring technological advances) as rollicking good times with copious albacore. This would not be a bad time to say thank you, once again, to Liz, who I assume was caring for our child while I enjoyed this rollicking good time.

If I was able to fish through fatherhood in previous falls, the move and the job are the next two culprits. The move is a convenient one. If I could heap all the responsibility for lost fishing time on the move, I could move on and not fear since I will not be moving again for the foreseeable future. My job as a teacher is more troubling as it has the potential to last decades. For years I steamed at friends who always had to work when we should have been fishing. They were friends who for the most part lived in central New Jersey and held office jobs. Fishing for them meant plane rides and vacation days, whereas I could be fishing in a matter of minutes, a three hour window was just about all I needed for a worthwhile outing, yet I could scarcely seem to find the time.

But I do not think the fall was lost to any one of the above. Neither a move, nor a job, nor the existence of an offspring was responsible in and of itself. A perfect storm of responsibilities conspired to keep a rod out of my hand, and I can live with that. But failing to acknowledge that the conditions of my life are now ripe for such storms would be putting my head in the sand.

Instead of ignoring the fact that fishing seasons are now in peril, which they most certainly are, comfort must come by looking to what was gained in creating a life that can snatch an entire season from me. One time I was going somewhere with Chick, I was driving and he was in his car-seat, and I looked at him in the rearview and my eyes filled with tears and I had to pull over. I do not remember how old he was, or where we were going, or why, there was nothing noteworthy about any of it. Just the sight of him overfilled me with happiness and appreciation. Thankfully, I am not brought to tears too often, but I still get the same type of feeling sometimes. I get it watching Chick play on the floor, or I get it watching him eat his lunch. I am even more likely to get it when he talks to me, when he says something like, "I have bacon and pancakes and syrup and mac and cheese and chicken soup and chocolate milk and cookies for breakfast, okay Daddy?" and looks at me with a charming, yet conspiratorial, smile, like he will not tell Mom about the cookies. I get it sometimes in the car, just checking on him in the rear-view, as he smiles and looks out the window. In particular, while driving, I have to try and keep my love for him in check so I do not run us off the road.

At times like these, sometimes I think to say, "I love you Chick," and he is likely to give me look, probably very similar to the one I give his mother in moments I feel she is being overly emotional, and say, "I whove you too Dada," in a declarative tone that suggests the issue was never in question and it was slightly silly of me to bring it up. Of course, that kind of response sends me right to the edge of some kind of physical breakdown.

Fishing has given me plenty of moments of profound happiness and acute appreciation. I have looked around many flats, many beaches, many expanses of ocean and thought to myself, *this is a pretty sweet life.* Fishing has provided me with more excitement, shown me more natural beauty and given me more smiles than any one man is entitled to, but it never brought me to tears. The phenomena of parenting, the deep connection to, appreciation of, and love I have for Chick is not something that can be replicated with a fly rod or a circle-hook rigged ballyhoo. The symptoms are downright injurious, but the cause is pure magic. The fall was lost to love, and if you are going to lose a fall, love is the best possible reason.

My fishing nut lifestyle, easily maintained as a bachelor, has been under attack for years. It probably could have withstood homeownership and a career forever. It cannot stand against love, and any teetering vestiges may have been vanquished toward the end of the lost fall. On November 6th, at four in the morning, my daughter Vivian was born.

Right now, everybody is too sleepy to contemplate the big changes. At the very least, we have signed ourselves up for another two-plus years of diapers, who knows how many sleep-deprived days and nights, and a few more years of providing some kind of direct supervision to not one but two children, and failing that, at least arranging for some. My plan for taking Chick fishing some days to relieve his mother, and then fishing during the reciprocal days off is completely shot to hell (at least until Vivian is old enough to fish). I am forward thinking enough to have booked my mother-in-law into childcare help for February school vacation, and booked myself off to Costa Rica along with Mike and Bill, a trip I now look forward to for a portion of every single day, but beyond that, I do not know when and how my fishing is going to happen.

My buddy Paul and I do not talk too frequently, but we do exchange emails and phone calls on a semi-regular basis. Until recently, the topic was usually if he was available for a fishing trip, and him saying no, but I will not be sending another email like that for a while (though April school vacation is nice a time to be bonefishing, and I wonder if my mother-in-law is available). In any case, after an unusually lengthy silence from him, particularly peculiar because I had inquired about his availability for the Costa Rica trip, I got word. His exhaustion and weariness were as evident in the sparse text of his email as if we had met face to face. His circumstances had changed in exactly the same way mine had, a new house, a new job and going from one child to two, in quick succession. He apologized for being incommunicado, said he was out for Costa Rica. Being a basketball player, he offered the explanation that life changes drastically when you have to switch from the double team to straight man-to-man.

Even more often now, while sitting around my living room, with my now family of four, I am struck with appreciation. Little Vivi will be snoozing in her mother's arms and Chick will be playing with his toys on the floor or sitting with me watching cartoons, the chaos of our days gives way for a few moments, I will lapse into a state of serenity. Surely, I am emerging with the most complete happiness of my life.

Building this life is hours upon hours of hard, not necessarily appealing work, hopefully leading to sublime moments that make it all worthwhile. You change thousands of diapers, tell your child "no" ten thousand times, cook an extra few hundred dinners because they will only eat mac and cheese, perform countless other tasks, for less frequent moments when your child smiles at you, or tells you he loves you, or states something so funny or ridiculous or profound that you fall in love with them all over again.

In that respect, it is not all that different from fishing; it is not unlike cast after cast after cast in the roaring Atlantic, poling across a big flat, driving around a big ocean staring at and occasionally tinkering with your trolling spread, or staying up late crimping or twisting leaders. Plenty of time and energy is dedicated to activities not desirable in and of themselves in hope of a payoff in the form of a hook-up and then a catch. The true fishing nut, though, will find some kind of pleasure in the whole process. As John Gierach says, "catching a fish is the goal, but not necessarily the point." The success of a fishing trip should not be judged by the size or number of the catch; something is gained from every step, or at least many steps, along the way. In addition to the large and obvious moments of happiness, the hook-up and eventual landing, there are many small perhaps even unconscious, moments of joy and beauty on a fishing trip: a tight loop in your fly line as it sails ninety feet, the waving emerald eel grass on the bottom of the flat, a glimpse of two happy bluefish cruising in three feet of crystal clear water along Point Rip, the sunrise over Smith's Point on a Bonito Bar morning. All fall short of supremely satisfying, yet they provide happiness and certainly contribute immeasurably to the experience. It would surely be folly to overlook the moments of extreme action and satisfaction when looking at what shapes a fishing trip, but it would be equally foolish to overlook the more subtle appearances of beauty or perfection. The same may be true of parenting. There are moments of pure elation but that is not the whole story. In order to create a happiness that endures, the moments of pure elation must be woven with restrained appearances of fulfillment and beauty and satisfaction derived from the process and the experience rather than just the result.

Another consideration is that the intensity of the happiness and satisfaction are directly proportionate to the hard work. For instance, you could catch a striper by finding yourself on Nantucket, strolling down to Straight Wharf and signing up for some striper fishing with a charter boat. Your captain and mate drive you to Sankaty while you sip a beer and eat a sandwich. Upon arrival you are handed large rod with wire line that has already been let out for you, and you are told to move it back and forth with enthusiasm. Before long, your rod doubles over forcefully, and after a short yet arduous fight against the fish (and the tackle, and the boat continually moving forward to make sure the line stays tight and you do not lose it), the mate nets a respectable striper, and throws him in the box. You sip another beer on your way home, enjoy beautiful scenery, eat fresh fish for dinner and have yourself a supremely agreeable day.

Or, you could catch a striper by getting a fly rod and learning to cast it in your back yard over several winter evenings and weekends, learning to tie flies and tying deceiver after deceiver until one looks as good as the picture in the catalog, reading about striped bass, fly fishing for striped bass, and everything else that seems relevant, making your way to Nantucket, walking beaches and wading the flats north of Eel Point for hours, and then, upon seeing a shadow moving along the bottom, casting your deceiver in front of it. Perhaps there have been many shadows and many fish to this point, or maybe this is your first encounter, at this point it matters little. You watch it turn, you strip and it eats your fly, and you set the hook. After a spirited run away from you, the fish turns back and you panic for a moment, then begin stripping again rather than reeling to keep the line tight, and then panic again when the fish changes direction and you hope the loose line shooting back out the guides does not find your foot, a button, the reel handle, or anything else that could cause enough resistance for your tippet to part. After the second run, in which the line went out thankfully free of obstruction, you coax the fish in gradually, hold him by the lip as you slip the fly out, and let him swim away. In both cases, the result is catching a striper, but it is plain as day that one will be more rewarding and profound in the life of the angler.

Maybe family life and parenting are rewarding not in spite of the difficulty, but instead, precisely because they are difficult. I am the type of angler who learned to cast a fly rod, ties his own flies, and wades the flats. Even if it means a lost season or three, I will be the same type of dad.

I do not know what the future holds, who knows how many fishing trips will be skipped, cancelled or never even scheduled. Who knows how many entire seasons will be lost. I know it will be crazier than a quadruple sailfish hookup. Some days will be longer than a fishless bluefin trip that begins at two-thirty in the morning. It will be tougher than permit on fly. And it will be worth it.

About the Author

Matt Reinemo was born on Nantucket and lives there with his wife Liz, son Chick, and daughter Vivian. He has been a fishing guide for sixteen seasons, and he is new to teaching eighth grade social studies. In addition to juggling family life and fishing, Matt enjoys cooking and racquet sports. *Fishing Nantucket: A Guide for Island Anglers* is Matt's first book, and *Compass of My Soul: Essays from a Fishing Nut Navigating Family Life* is his second.

Matt loves to hear from readers, contact him to set up a fishing trip or just drop him a line:
email: **fishingnantucket@gmail.com**
website: **www.fishingnantucket.com**

You can also follow Matt on social media:
Facebook: **www.facebook.com/FishingNantucket**
Twitter: **@MattReinemo**

Made in the USA
Monee, IL
28 January 2021